Discovering
My Life's Purpose

From Tragedy to Triumph

BRIDGID M. RUDEN, ARNP

ISBN 978-1-68197-199-5 (Paperback)
ISBN 978-1-68197-200-8 (Digital)

Copyright © 2016 by Bridgid M. Ruden, ARNP

Editor: Ana King
Cover Design and painting angel copyright © Barbara Schreiber.
All Rights Reserved.

Christian Faith Publishing, Inc.
296 Chestnut Street
Meadville, PA 16335
www.christianfaithpublishing.com

Printed in the United States of America

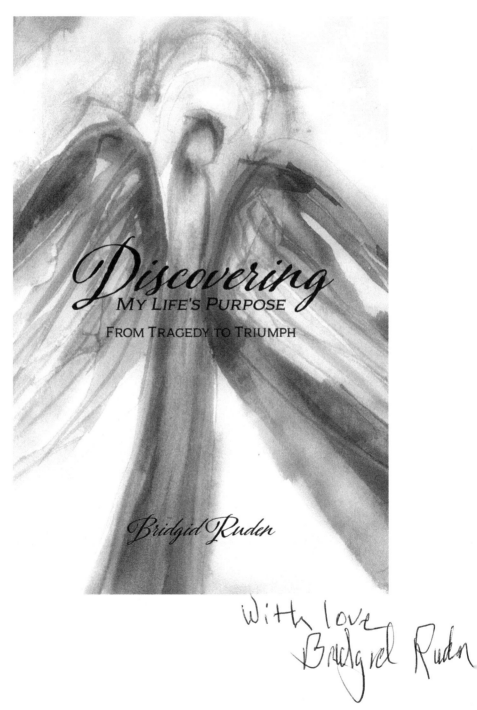

Discovering
MY LIFE'S PURPOSE
FROM TRAGEDY TO TRIUMPH

Bridgid Ruden

With love
Bridgid Ruden

This book is dedicated to my amazing husband, children, family, my friends, colleagues, advocates, and anyone who has experienced suffering.

ACKNOWLEDGEMENTS

Due to memory loss and cognitive challenges which are secondary to my traumatic brain injury, writing this story was very challenging. My family, friends, colleagues, and health professionals have significantly helped me find my way through the reflection of time that has passed and where I stand today. I can't begin to say how extremely grateful I am as this book would not have been written without their love and support.

One of the most divine healing women in my life, my sister-in-law Lori, states: *"Bridgid, your passion has been a blessing for the many people you have touched. You continue to be a powerful healer. You are an inspiration and a light worker. I know you still have your challenges, but I see you as whole. The essence of your beautiful spirit continues to be one who shares, loves, teaches and ultimately helps others to heal."*

—Lori Hemesath

CONTENTS

INTRODUCTION

It may seem strange to you, my readers, to begin this book by sharing in the first chapter some poems that were written at the time of my birth. But it was suggested to me by an editor from the University of Iowa College of Arts that writing about my life from my birth forward would help me to recall important experiences and the impact they had on discovering my life's purpose. I have found this to be true. While writing this book, my mind has been flooded with memories. Hopefully, as I put them in writing, they will give you and me a good picture of who I was before my accident and who I have become.

All that I can remember from my bicycle ride on May 24, 2008, is a gentle ride in the early morning with my dear friend Angie Cookman. Soon I was lying at the bottom of a hill, helmet cracked, bleeding from my ear. Based on my behavior and appearance, Angie knew this was not a mild concussion as she was told by a police officer. I was in danger and needed emergency care. The next days, weeks, months, and now years have challenged me—first to simply survive, and then to heal physically and emotionally, and ultimately to redefine my life in such a way that it has new meaning and purpose.

Thank you for joining me on my journey of discovery.

CHAPTER 1

Poetry Created at Birth

I was born into a Catholic family, the oldest of eight children. My beautiful mother, Jeananne, is an Irish lass with a classy maiden name of Callahan. The name Callahan noted in the website www.babynames.com is an Irish name interpreted as "a little bright-headed one who is supportive of a church." My heart soars knowing that I am 75 percent Irish, a valued contribution to my upbringing. People have said that my Irish heritage has contributed to my courage, spunk, and determination—something that was sorely needed in my journey of discovery.

As I entered this world, a nurse named Loie, with whom mom worked in obstetrics, was wonderfully present during my birth at Xavier Hospital in Dubuque, Iowa. Loie was an outstanding nurse. As a gift to my mother, Loie wrote an amazing poem commemorating my birth. My mother shared this poem with me many years ago. It has always made me smile.

On St. Valentine's Day of '64 God
had something special in store.
A sweetheart was in His plan, special
delivery to Don and Jeananne.
The clock on the wall said 2:53 when
along came me...Bridgid Marie.
I'm filled with wrinkles and bounces and
I tipped the scales at 6 pounds 6 ounces.
The next statistic, now don't you laugh
but my measurement is 20 1/2.
I'm cute and cuddly with a turned up nose.
I have the required number of fingers
and toes. My hair is a deep dark brown
and just as soft as thistle down.
My dark eyes sparkle with glee because
my parents are thrilled with me.

My paternal great-grandmother Mamie also
wrote a poem after I was born. Mamie was a home
health nurse who specialized in delivering babies.

Ode to Baby

You came like the fair faint flush of dawn
Like the rose pure love in your heart
Like a breath that is breathed in Heaven
Of that Heaven, a beautiful part.

All round you gleamed love that is holy,
Like fragrance that roses bestow
The velvet touch of your dimpled hand
Divinity a mother and daddy must know.

14

You came by neither plane nor train,
Loved ones here paid all your fare;
Coming on skids of everlasting love, God guided you
With Angels who lived with you up there.

You came to a world of puzzles and care
But to God and yourself, remain true
Your good Irish name and good Irish gist
Will help you fight your way through.

Together we'll dance an old Irish Jig
Surely hearts of Callahan's and Freymann's must gleam
Then pass each one a good Irish swig
And together we'll sing "The Wearin' o' The Green."
Not for gold or for the whole wide world
Would Don and Jan ever dare to part
With the thrill that you brought with you
When you found a home in each loving heart.

With all this attention surrounding my birth, I have now come to believe I was born with a special purpose.

CHAPTER 2

The Early Years: A Young Nurse in Training

At a young age, I embraced opportunities to care for and heal whoever needed me. When I was three to four years old, Aunt Eileen, my dad's sister in Seattle, brought us kids hamsters in her purse on the plane. Mom already had three children and wasn't too happy about this potential chaos entering our busy home. I was very fond of taking care of them. I enjoyed feeding and watering them and watching them race. I was not afraid of hamsters. When they scrambled around the spinner, my mother had a hard time sleeping due to the dreadful noise. Often they escaped from the porch and into the small house. My brother Brian and I diligently searched many tiny areas looking for the rodents. Mom was terrified of rodents. Hilariously, Mom hides a fake mouse where we least expect it!

Early in grade school, I tried to help any animal that was suffering. In second grade I shared with a good friend that someday I would be a nurse. I frequently crossed a busy street near my house to explore a beautiful grove of trees. One time I found a newborn bird that had fallen from its nest. Determined to return it to its nest, I climbed the tall tree holding this frail baby bird. The mother bird made a warning screech. I continued my mission, climbing the high tree with small branches, once almost falling. When I approached the nest, the mother bird screeched again and scrambled along the branch. This frightened me so. Out of fear, I placed the bird on the same branch and climbed back down the tree in a hurry. The mother's power and determination reminds me now of my own mother. To this day, I still think about that baby bird and hope that it survived. Interestingly, I still adore birds. I feed them fruit and nut seed which is what they love. This type of seed attracts Midwestern birds that I've never seen before, such as the rose-breasted grosbeak. When the birdfeeder is empty I head outside with the bird seed and instinctively say to them, "Momma's here." My kids would flip out if they heard me.

We had a variety of stray cats coming and going from our home. Cats were precious to me. My mischievous brother once pushed a black cat down a metal laundry chute from the top of our two-story home down to the basement and even tried to put the cat in the dryer! The cat frequently bit us showing disdain, fear, and anger. Father John O'Connor, my mother's cousin, frequently visited our home. He displayed a rough personality to us children. Father O'Connor took the cat in his car and supposedly dropped it off in a field. I truly feared he shot the cat. Such a symbol of life's circumstances, over which I have no control.

One day my father brought home four young mallard ducks. The four of us children cared for them until we could safely take them to a pond. They initially lived in one small pool downstairs and as they became old enough they were placed in our small back yard pool. We enjoyed feeding them grain. One day when I checked on them, only three mallards were present. My siblings and I searched all around our yard and neighborhood for the missing duck. We found him torn apart and dead. Neighbors said that a dog killed him. We arose in fury and hurried to try and find this dog. I was so angry and sad for the unnecessary death of that precious mallard duck! When the three remaining ducks were grown we took them to a pond to be with other mallards. We gently let them go to witness their enthusiasm as they swam away grateful and excited to be where they belonged.

Since I enjoyed caring for animals, I was allowed to keep another hamster, Snow White, a white-haired and red-eyed hamster that became frightened when folks looked at her. Her white hair with red eyes seemed to scare those who met her for the first time. Several times she escaped from her cage. I wondered if my brothers purposely let her escape! Eventually I would find her and she appeared to do well despite leaving home. One day I found her lying so quietly in her cage. She wasn't moving or breathing at all. She had died, which brought me much sadness. Why or how did this happen?

Burying her in a small casket outside was very important to me. Looking around the house, I found a Pringles container and gently placed her in there with a couple of paper towels. I left this on the kitchen counter as I went outside to dig her grave. My mom and my maternal grandmother, Ann Callahan, who had come to visit us, were not aware of this. Grandma Callahan often made cookies and stored them in a Pringles container for storage. She attempted to

remove the cookies from the Pringles container and out slid
a very dead hamster. Grandma screamed. At first I thought
that she may be alive as she sort of displayed a slight movement. Was she truly alive? Was I crazy? I was not thinking
properly. I neglected to understand Grandma's fear even
though a dead hamster flew out of a Pringles container!

I continued to prepare for her burial. A wonderful
family friend, Father Walz, was visiting our home. He was
informed about this traumatic situation. He met me outside when I was ready to bury her. Father prayed for her
and helped me bury her. This was very kind of him to support this event. I never asked to have a hamster again. This
was too painful to re-experience. My maternal grandfather,
Walter, a hard working farmer, told me that he would get
me a horse if I helped my mother take care of my siblings. This motivated me as I had always dreamed of own-
ing and caring for a horse. Although I helped my mother
to the best of my ability, my dream didn't come true. So
I turned my attention to wishing for a young chimpanzee monkey. Of course I never got a chimpanzee either.

Not only did I love caring for animals, but also for people. So, I trained to be a Candy Striper for the local hospital.
I delivered flowers and gift items to the hospital patients.
No, not a stripper, as this is the word I read when I visualize
striper. When my sister Rachel was six years old, she loved
jumping up from a picnic table to the swing set bar and
swirling like a gymnast. On one occasion, after making some
red Kool-Aid, she wiped her hands with a wet washcloth
and headed outside to jump on the swing set. Rachel leaped
from a distance and tried to grab the bar. Her hands slid and
she smashed hard into the ground. Her screams let me know
what tremendous pain she was experiencing. Her left arm
was out of position. With love and compassion I stayed with

her. It was as if I knew how to proceed. I created a sling from a towel to help secure her arm and provided ice to reduce the swelling. Somehow, my brother and I made it to the hospital but I can't picture anyone else being there. I believe I was with her before and after her surgery. The left elbow had a compound fracture and three pins were placed in it.

From this time forward, in sixth grade I started babysitting infants and those in grade school. I worked as often as I could. Not only did I love babysitting, I also valued earning money. I was the oldest of eight children and by this time needed some income. When I was in high school, some of my friends came over to my house for a visit one day. When they ventured into my home they were shocked to see four of my siblings ill and vomiting on the kitchen floor. Always resourceful, I provided each with an empty gallon ice cream container. My friends laughed hysterically. I couldn't leave my siblings, Brian, Kathleen, Rachel, and Peter, alone. Therefore, my friends tried to help me and it became an adventure! My life's purpose was emerging, which is to take care of others, especially children.

CHAPTER 3

An Amazing Man Enters My Life

In the summer of 1983, Todd Ruden and I met while we were both working as counselors at Albrecht Acres Camp for adults and children with special needs. When I first saw Todd, my eyes widened, my breathing deepened, and my heart started racing. Todd was *gorgeous*! Not only was Todd good looking, but he had a real gift for interacting beautifully with people with disabilities. I always wished that we could be partners in some of the activities that required a team approach. But we were never assigned to work on the same team. In my opinion, the head counselor was interested in Todd herself which may have had something to do with my never being assigned to work with him all summer. On one occasion, several of the counselors were hanging out with the campers during an activity break. One young girl looked at Todd and me sitting near each other at a picnic table. She said, "You two should always be together." Children can be so very intuitive.

But nothing happened between us for several years. Then I initiated contact when my sister Kathleen started dating a guy whom Todd knew from Dubuque, Iowa, and I wanted to know Todd's opinion of him. After getting some feedback for my sister, Todd asked me out on a date once he determined that I wasn't dating anyone else special at the time. He took me to a restaurant on our first date. We both felt as though we were the only two people in the restaurant. The waiter had to return to our table multiple times to see if we were ready to order our food. We were captivated with each other. Todd recalls thinking that my green eyes were stunning. Todd and I got married on November 3, 1990. We would eventually have three children together and a life that was both fulfilling and challenging.

Todd is an electrical engineer and Program Manager at Rockwell Collins. Todd is such a kind, patient, calm, educated, and nurturing man and an amazing son, husband, father, and friend. In my eyes, he is an earth angel who has held our family together when we have been faced with difficult circumstances. Norene, Todd's mother, expresses that every mother has hopes and dreams for her little boy as he grows into a man. Todd has not only fulfilled all of these hopes and dreams, he has surpassed them. Norene especially loves his sense of humor, his generosity toward others, and his loyalty to family and friends. Todd works and plays hard and he has become a success in everything he does. A poem written by Todd's father, Dick, is entitled ***"What Makes a Man Remarkable?"***

It's his character, and the way he treats people.
It's his sense of loyalty, and the
way he's there for loved ones
It's his generous heart, and love of friends
and family…
It's more than what he does, it's who he is.

My parents describe Todd as "a man who has shown his ability to be strong, self-directed, supportive of his wife and family, always encouraging, gently guiding, determined to seek good outcomes, playful, protective, fun loving, patient, courageous, tender hearted, encouraging and lovable. We have witnessed these abilities when he was faced with difficult decisions, family matters and setbacks in your recovery. We are so grateful for his loving endurance. Todd was steadfast in his strength—a real family hero."

C H A P T E R   4

A Bright Nursing Career Unfolds

In 1986, I graduated from Mt. Mercy College in Cedar
Rapids, Iowa with a Bachelor of Science Degree in Nursing
(BSN). When I began seeing patients for the first time
while still in college, I was scared but drawn since child-
hood to caring for the young. My first nursing experience within a hospital setting was caring for pediatric
patients. My nursing instructor stated, "Bridgid, you provide wonderful care to pediatric patients. Is this your calling?" My first position as a nurse was at Mayo Clinic in
Rochester, Minnesota. I had the privilege of caring for
pediatric and adult patients recovering from cardiac surgery. I adored working with the pediatric population.

After getting married and having my first child, I
returned to college to work on a master's degree. In 1994, I
achieved a Master of Science degree and in 1995, certifica-
tion as an Advanced Registered Pediatric Nurse Practitioner

(ARNP). Both were obtained from the University of Iowa College of Nursing. Achieving this amazed me. Further education was challenging while working and raising a child. In addition, I was Adjunct Faculty and Clinical Instructor at the University of Iowa College of Nursing. In this role, I provided nursing students a clinical practicum working with the pediatric population suffering from a cardio-pulmonary condition.

In addition, I also worked as a nurse in the Pediatric Oncology department. During this time, I wrote an article entitled "Bereavement Follow-Up: An Opportunity to Extend Nursing Care." This was written to extend nursing care beyond the hospital setting and embrace the loss, abandonment, and grief the bereaved family experienced after losing a child to cancer. In addition, I created a focus group of hematology nurses who, in turn, created a bereavement support group for families of the child for whom they provided care. This grief support group validated and honored their loss beyond one year after the death, as many believe that grief has truly lessened after this time. The support group further educated nurses on the necessity of staying in touch with the patient's family to reduce their suffering and loss.

I was an active participant in grant funding for children and published several articles. The articles or booklet varied in the areas in which I was working. In 2003, while working as a pediatric nurse practitioner in the school district, I began speaking for the first time to nursing students, health care professionals, and school teachers regarding asthma in the pediatric population. I created a booklet entitled *Asthma Education and Management in the School Setting*. In addition, I taught asthmatic children the Open Airways program, coordinated Asthma 101 trainings for school nurses, initiated an indoor air quality team, and managed asthma grants from the American Association of School Administrators and the American Lung Association.

I was a resource person for family practice residents, school nurses and health secretaries. While I was working as a nurse practitioner, many children and adolescents I cared for were uninsured and thus without a health care provider. I was very fortunate to provide health care in free medical clinics, including the Visiting Nurses Association, school-based health care, and community health resources. In addition, I worked with pregnant and parenting adolescents and their children via home or school visitation. Many children came from single parent homes in which the parents were often unemployed. On occasion, one of the parents was incarcerated. I saw some devastating things. These children touched my soul. I'm privileged to have worked with them. Susie Green, a facilitator of Metro Care Connection, and my colleague and dear friend, once told me that I was the person who she witnessed providing health care with concern, compassion, smiles, laughter, empowerment, and education to children, families, and school educators.

CHAPTER 5

Tragedy

When I was five years old, my dad taught me how to ride a bike. He held onto the seat as I was pedaling and jogged alongside me. I assumed he continued to hold on as I pedaled. But like any parent, he taught me how to ride, believed in my ability, and let me go. Riding alone was a thrill! Such tremendous joy and determination emerged. I loved riding a bike and a mystical spirit emerged within me. We never wore helmets back then. One time in grade school, I fell off a bike and injured my leg. Yes, I experienced pain, blood, and bruising, but that didn't stop me. The best adventures occurred when I rode on wonderful bike riding trails that were surrounded by nature.

Knowing how much I enjoyed bike riding, two nurse practitioner colleagues in neonatology encouraged me to join them on a triathlon in 2008. One of these women was an incredible runner and the other was overall athletic. But

I would be a newcomer to competition at that level. I was skeptical when I listened to my colleague's encouragement. I began to reflect on never succeeding at track in high school or making the volleyball team. As an adolescent, I was thin and poorly developed and hated showering in the women's bathroom following volleyball or basketball. I was convinced that God had forgotten about physically developing me. Lisa, a dear friend, also experienced such a disheartening struggle during puberty. I frequently read the book *Are You There God, It's Me Marga*ret by Judy Bloom. Margaret knew how I felt. Margaret intrigued me as she struggled with the same puberty issues that I did. We altered some of the lyrics to the song "Misfits" from the movie *Rudolph the Red-Nosed Reindeer*: "I am just but a misfit, nothing but a misfit. Just because my chest is flat, why don't I fit in?" My dear Grandma Bede, my paternal grandmother, sensed my pain and said, "Bridgid, your time will come."

As an adult, I ran 5K races and rode my bike on the Register's Annual Great Bicycle Ride Across Iowa (RAGBRAI) the largest bike touring event in the world, with my friend Angie Cookman. We went eighty-seven miles in two days. This was my first adventure during an incredibly hot July. One year, I pedaled forty-three miles in one day, on my own but without fear. When I completed this adventure, my dad cheered me on. But these activities were more fun-based than a triathlon. My brother Brian reminded me that in the eighth grade I won the Presidential Physical Fitness Award after competing in a 50-, 220-, and 600-yard dash, sit–ups, and flexed arm hangs. My dad taught me how to effectively accomplish these. Dad would take me outside to practice running as I scrambled in the dark around the house! Why on earth was I running in the dark?

I succeeded in clinical practice with wonderful nurse practitioners; couldn't I further master my athletic ability? The swimming component of a triathlon elevated my heart rate. I could swim but not in a manner to compete against a group of people. Training for the swimming component was the most challenging. But a trainer helped me immensely so that I could swim more effectively in a recreational pool and then in a river. The trainer believed in me and my colleagues continued encouraging me, which caused me to press on even though I was forty-four years of age. I was still in training for the triathlon when my bicycle accident occurred. According to the Centers for Disease Control and Prevention, the leading cause of traumatic brain injury includes: 1) Falls (35.2%), 2) Motor vehicle or traffic accidents (17.3%), 3) Struck by or against objects (16.5%), 4) Assaults (10%) and others, including sports injury, military blast injury.

On May 24, 2008, I casually rode my bike in the early morning with beautiful sunshine. I was headed on a fourteen-mile paved trail in Coralville, Iowa, with my dear friend Angie. Angie and I first met when our youngest children Molly and Maddy attended preschool together. We were thrilled there wasn't any rain that morning. Since I had been on vacation, I was excited to see her. So much to share and biking would provide this opportunity. Angie thought I should wait until the trail was wider for us to visit. We came to an area with a steep downward and upward hill; we were not speeding and were both wearing helmets. I had a new road bike with biking shoes clipped into the pedals. I only remember crossing a train track and then a hill appeared. At the bottom of the hill there was a large section of thick mud from poor drainage from fields nearby.

Angie heard me scream when I hit the muddy area. I moved side to side while still on the bike and then lost control and slammed the right side of my head onto the concrete. Despite this, both my shoes were still attached to the pedals and my helmet was trying so hard to cover my brain. Later, it was determined that the helmet was cracked all the way through, one to two inches on the right side. I immediately passed out and started bleeding immensely from my right ear and nose. Angie was twenty to thirty feet behind me and rode down the hill to be by my side. A woman from Pennsylvania was walking on the trail early that morning. She had a cell phone and called 911. Thank God, as Angie and I didn't usually carry a cell phone.

Angie stayed near me and was very troubled by the sight of me. Three to four feet alongside the trail were grass and weeds. Angie wished that I had been thrown to that area instead of directly onto the concrete. A police officer showed up first and reached for gauze to minimize continuous bleeding from my nose. He proceeded to downplay the medical situation in an attempt to reduce Angie's trauma. The police officer informed Angie several times that I had a slight concussion, but Angie knew that it was much worse. The ambulance was taking a long time to get there. Angie assumed it was hard for the ambulance to find the exact location, which only increased her anxiety, knowing I was in grave danger.

When I arrived at University of Iowa Hospital Emergency Treatment Center, I was in and out of consciousness and suddenly began to vomit. I wore a neck brace as I had a fracture of the C6 (cervical spinal injury) and a broken right clavicle. My husband Todd and my eleven-year-old son Ryan were able to reach the emergency room after notification from Jennifer Baker, a friend and colleague. My daughter Meghan, who was fourteen years old at the time, and a girl friend were playing on the computer and daughter Molly, age eight, was sound asleep at home.

Normal Brain CT   1st CT

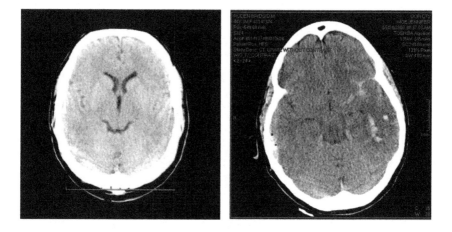

The neurosurgeon, Dr. Tim Ryken, was present and talked to Todd about my CT scan (CT is a Computerized Tomography, an x-ray that produced images that visualize internal structures in cross section). The CT scan revealed that the right side of my skull was fractured with a small amount of internal bleeding (right temporal epidural hematoma). A fist-sized epidural hematoma, a large blood clot, was caused by a fracture above and beyond my right ear. Also, my left temporal lobe was bruised and bleeding and the center was swollen. View the picture of a brain below to visualize various parts of the brain.

Regions of the Human Brain

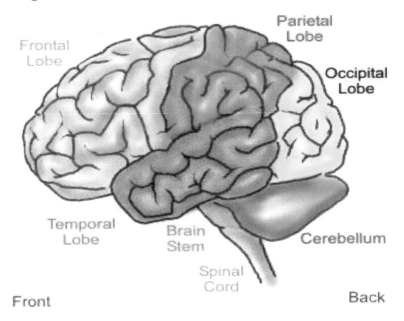

Dr. Ryken advised immediate surgery to remove my left skull bone flap to release internal pressure and allow my brain to swell. One physician in charge of the operating room told Dad that it was very unusual to have an operating room readily available on a Saturday morning. For this reason, they had plenty of time to prepare the operating room for my surgery. Some of the nursing staff in the operating room were those I previously educated in the Iowa College of Nursing. When my friend Jennifer was in the Intensive Care Unit (ICU), she talked with Dr. Ryken. Years prior, Jennifer and I worked with Dr. Ryken while he was a neurosurgical resident. In a state of dismay, he shared with Jennifer, "Based on the vision of her CT, this brain damage doesn't appear as if it occurred from a bicycle accident, it resembles injury from a car accident!"

On the first day of such devastation, Todd was shocked, numb, and not sure how on earth to proceed. Our son Ryan, who had come to the hospital with him, was confused and frightened. Todd thought at that time that I would be in the hospital for a week, but my body disagreed! After the first surgery was completed, my left pupil began to dilate. Not a good sign. The CT below demonstrates the left bone flap was removed to allow the brain to swell sufficiently. The left temporal side was now bruising. The right temporal blood clot enlarged and caused compression and shift of the midline. A second emergency surgery was needed and the hematoma was removed and the torn blood vessel was cauterized.

2nd CT scan

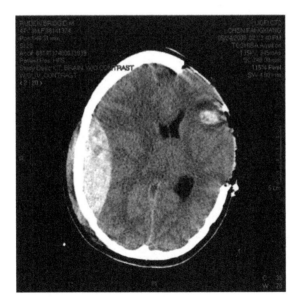

The following notes were made by Timothy Ryken, MD, the neurosurgeon who was on duty when I arrived at the hospital.

It should have been just another Saturday for the University of Iowa Neurosurgery Service. Typically this would include morning rounds, a resident teaching conference and a chance to catch up on the weekly paperwork while hoping for a quiet weekend.

But as we were finishing rounds and heading for the conference room, Bridgid Ruden, a young wife, mother and intensive care nurse, was strapping on her bicycle helmet for an early morning ride.

One slippery curve and one emergency transport later, now Bridgid Ruden lay with declining consciousness in the University of Iowa Emergency Room.

While her bike helmet likely saved her life, significant trauma was evident on her emergent imaging studies and her level of consciousness deteriorated even as I updated her husband on her condition.

Her brain showed signs of serious swelling in response to the trauma and an emergent operation was planned to temporarily remove a portion of the skull to allow the pressure to be relieved and let the blood flow return to the brain.

The Emergency Room and Operating Room personnel as well as the Neurosurgical team functioned efficiently and she was taken to the operating room where a decompressive craniectomy was undertaken.

But something was not right.

Despite removal of the bone, the brain continued to swell. Typically at this point the brain should have been relaxed. Having experienced this in the past, I suspected the worst. By alleviating the pressure on one side of the brain, a source of bleeding which was previously compressed was now causing a large blood clot to accumulate on the opposite side of the brain. Quickly confirming this with an emergent imaging study, we returned to the operating room to repeat the same operation on the opposite side of the brain and remove the blood clot.

Thankfully, at this point swelling appeared to be controlled. After updating the family, we all settled in for the anticipated long, slow recovery process.

Anyone familiar with neurological injury—whether from trauma, stroke or tumor—knows that recovery is slow and extremely variable. When the injury is bilateral the outcome is even less predictable.

The chance of the brain recovering consciousness following the onset of coma is highly variable. My mentor, and former Chairman of Neurosurgery at the University of Iowa, John VanGilder, MD, described the process as "reconnecting"—giving the impression of nerve cells trying to reconnect critical areas that had become "disconnected" as a result of trauma. As the process is still poorly understood, it has always seemed as reasonable as any description I have heard and I have found it helpful when attempting to describe the severe head injury recovery process to families.

Following the initial flurry of activity, the painful process of settling into the Intensive Care Unit routine began and all involved undertook the vigil of waiting for signs of neurological recovery. The story that follows is one of inspiration. The story that follows in one of a strong personal spirit and family support that needs to be told.

—Timothy Ryken, MD, Neurosurgeon

My parents and siblings were notified by phone. On this Memorial Day, my dad, Don Freymann, was playing golf with my two brothers, Andrew and Michael, and brother-in-law, Pat Lauer. They were golfing on the fifth tee at Bunker Hill Golf Course in Dubuque, Iowa. Following the dreaded phone call, Dad wondered if I was toe-clipped in on my bike. Chills ran through him. My toe clips remained on,

I was restricted from being thrown clear and free from the bike during a spill, which added severity to the accident.

Mom and Dad are practicing Catholics. They drove two hours praying the rosary until they reached Iowa City, Iowa. So many family members were called to pray for me. All were unsure of what I was experiencing. When my parents arrived at the hospital they went directly to the ICU. Dad was very anxious and afraid when he learned of the seriousness of my accident. Mom was shocked and feared the outcome. They were placed in a waiting room with many other people. Angie stated that the room looked like a campground filled with beverages and snacks. All were anticipating news of their loved ones.

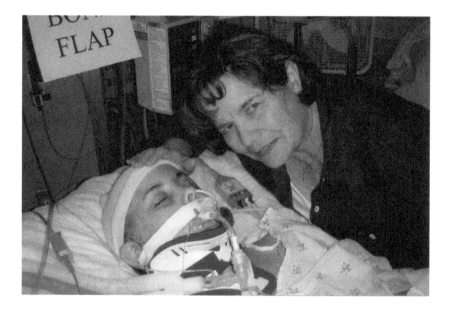

Dad's first glimpse of me was overwhelming. Immense fear ricocheted within him. "There lay our beautiful first-born child who had achieved so many good things and worked so hard to become a good nurse, mother and wife." My mother was afraid that she was losing me and needed to hold on to some part of me. While lying in a coma, mom's loving hand is powerfully holding my shattered skull. My incredible God-given mother, an earth angel, who always has and always will be by my side.

Not knowing if she was going to lose me, my mom asked health care providers, "Do you still have Bridgid's hair?" The hair was disposed of because it was soiled with blood and debris. Mom felt as if she were experiencing a wretched dream and yearned to believe that this was only a dream, not reality.

When the second emergency brain surgery took another four and a half hours, Dad's heart sank deeper. He wondered if I would die or be in a vegetative state for the rest of my life. This was almost too much for my parents to absorb. When I asked Dad later if he would share what he experienced during that time, he stated that it was too depressing a time for him to even reflect on. Mom knew they would open my right skull bone to remove a large hematoma. Her breath was taken away. She was speechless and scared.

When Molly arose she questioned where I was. A tremor emerged in Meghan when Todd told her that I was in a horrible bicycle accident. He expressed uncertainty as to what would occur. Meghan just stared at her dad, not believing a word he was saying. Many don't comprehend the magnitude of such a tragedy at the time it occurs.

Meghan, years later as a student at the University of Iowa, created an essay regarding her experience visiting me for the first time. When Meghan arrived at the hospital, she didn't know what to expect. She entered the waiting room hearing her relatives' sniffling noses and viewing their puffy eyes. Meghan internally felt like saying, "Oh God." I was much worse than what Todd had told her. Meghan's maternal grandfather, Don, wanted to go into my room with her. He held her closely as they slowly entered my room. She immediately broke down and began sobbing. The woman in the coma was not the mother she knew. Meghan couldn't stand seeing me like that. All she could think of was "getting the hell out of there." She walked out of the room, sobbing, as aunts and uncles rushed to console her. Everything after that is just a blur for Meghan. She wandered around the hospital, trying not to panic or think about the consequences, but she was overcome by fear. Her heart felt numb not knowing whether I would live or die. Many doctors and nurses were expressing concern and offering support for our family. Several were my colleagues. After the second surgery, health care professionals alerted the family to the changes they should watch for in my neurological condition. They described the implications of various physiological and neurological alterations. My mother verbalized, "God help Bridgid and help me to be there for her and her family." There were hard days ahead and Mom tried very hard to stay in the moment. Her true tears never arose until she had the opportunity to travel back to her home in Dubuque for the first time. She was greeted by all her wonderful supportive friends who secured a place for Mom to truly express her emotions. Mom cried for as long and as hard as she ever has. With tears there is such release of the trauma she was experiencing and friendships to nurture her.

When my mother and father celebrated their fortieth anniversary, my siblings and I surprised them with a celebration. Such a joy to witness their utter shock as we were all gathered together to celebrate triumph. I wrote them the following poem, which embraces the celebration of their life together raising eight children and amazingly nine grandchildren. No one ever thought of the tremendous violation that could occur in their life's journey.

Generations of Love

On November 17, 1962
Mom and Dad joined souls
with the words, "I do".
The day was chilly but love warmed the air
as friends and family gathered at St.
Anthony's to celebrate this pair.

Mom wore a dress patterned in roses
and carried a single red rose.
Dad though dashing in his attire took
one look at mom and nearly froze.
Karen was the Maid of Honor
and Peter the Best Man.
The proud parents were Virgil,
Bede, Walter, and Ann.
All witnessed the marriage
that was in God's plan.

Time went on and miracles arrived when
the marriage was blessed with children:
Bridgid, Brian, Kathleen, and
Glen. Was this the end?
Oh me! Oh my! How time
flew as the family grew
when along came Rachel, Peter,
Michael, and Andrew!

Diapers, band-aids, stitches, casts,
Fights, tantrums, tears, and sass.
Ask anyone and they would have told,

there was never a dull moment in
the Freymann household.

How did they all survive you may ask?
Togetherness, tough love, and
angels continuously on task...
But that is past tense and another
generation of love has arrived at last
humbling the siblings who survived the past.

The new generation arrived so jolly:
Meghan, Alex, Ryan, Christian, and Molly.
This group continues to be blessed
with both gals and fellas
including Peter, Alejandra and
now Samuel and Ella.

This year Mom and Dad celebrate
forty years together.
Their commitment has endured
all kinds of weather.
They hung on to the marital roller coaster ride
willingly and lovingly, taking
ups and downs in stride.

And now can't you see the fruits
from the generations of love
all formed from a marriage destined
and blessed by heaven above?

With love and gratitude for
the gift of my parents.

Several people traveled great distances to be present with me and our family. Many were shocked, frightened and lost in trying to understand medical jargon and true results. In and of itself, denial emerged. Some couldn't believe the accident even had occurred. Family dynamics were altered and transformation was beginning. Todd's father, Dick Ruden was shocked, sad, and recollected how important and valuable family is in his life. He began praying even more than he had before. Norene, Todd's mother, says it still brings tears to her eyes, remembering how I looked the night of the accident. To her, I appeared fragile, tiny, and broken, as if I were a china doll that had fallen to the floor. She couldn't imagine me being in such a helpless condition. In her eyes, I was always healthy and fit and it was very difficult to see me in such a delicate condition.

Norene's mother, Grandma Faley, a precious ninety-three-year-old woman, was living alone in her home in Dubuque, Iowa. Grandma Faley, so kind and giving to so many people, treated me as if I were her own grandchild. During this time, she abruptly developed acute pancreatitis and required immediate surgery. Both of us were hospitalized and struggling for life. The combination of these situations was very stressful and required such a prayerful time for the Ruden family. In addition, it seemed the family history of brain trauma was unfortunately repeating itself. On July 4, 2000, my brother-in-law, Bill Hemesath, died of a glioblastoma, an aggressive malignant tumor of the brain.

Andee Steciw, RN, was one of the nurses who cared for me both in the intensive care and step-down unit. Andee honestly shared with my family that sometimes when nurses are working with a trauma patient they shut down their own emotions to maximize their focus on direct patient care. This is not a cold pathway but a necessity in order to stabilize patients and save their lives. In other words, they remove themselves from the patient's traumatic experience and lean toward in-depth work on their survival both to stabilize them and try to save their life. Andee remarked how very difficult it is for her to stay unbiased and emotionally separated from each patient she cares for as well as their troublesome story. I was one of Andee's patients from whom she had difficulty remaining emotionally detached. She visualized a healthy, fit lady training for a triathlon and exercising to achieve her fitness goals. Andee knew that my life and that of my family and friends had changed in a split second as I was fighting for my life. While she cared for me in the ICU, my physiological and neurological responses were very common for neurological trauma patients. Despite this, the brain trauma was very different from usual head traumas caused by bicycle accidents. I was wearing a helmet, not drinking or using drugs when this bad day struck. Andee questioned how this tragedy could even occur as I rode my bike effectively and properly with a helmet on and did everything right!

Many of the brain injured patients Andee works with head to the operating room several times, as I did. Family members often hear words like: "removing brain flaps," "high ICPs," "coma," and "they may never follow commands again." Health care professionals are trying hard to communicate what is occurring, yet families are in shock and aren't capable of hearing them. Often this is the worst day of their lives; their world is shattering. When Andee was working with me and my family, she was afraid that I would never survive this accident. Despite her fears, Andee always gave hope to patients and families tempered by reality. Once a patient is stable and able to leave ICU, the next challenge for a health care professional who pours his/her heart and soul into the patient's care is to "let go," not knowing the long-term outcome for the patient.

I was in a coma, a state of unconsciousness that lasts more than six hours during which I was unable to consciously hear, speak, feel, or move. A Glasgow Coma Scale is a way to measure consciousness, especially after brain injury. I had the value of a six on the Glasgow Coma Scale when I arrived in the emergency room (the best level is fifteen) and it rapidly deteriorated until I was comatose. The Glascow Coma Scale is administered numerous times per day and the numerical scores are based on a patient's ability to open their eyes, respond verbally, and begin some physical motor function. Did I follow commands on the last neurological exam they performed? How about today? Will I truly continue to follow commands and venture out of this coma, ever? My nurse, Andee would pinch me to ascertain if I would have a physiological response. She constantly watched the pupils within my eyes for any alteration. She often asked questions like, "Bridgid, can you wiggle your toes?" "Bridgid, please open your eyes, so I know you're hearing me." Andee wondered if I was truly following her commands or just exhibiting a reflexive movement. If Andee thought I followed a simple command, she would keep this to herself with great hope that I would do it again before she could ever comfortably tell my family. She hated to give false hope.

Following my initial surgery, I required a breathing tube, feeding tube, two Hemovacs (drainage tubes to remove any bleeding or fluid), percutaneous intravenous lines (an IV placed in a major blood vessel leading to the heart), and a Foley catheter. Patients who have experienced neurological trauma as I did demonstrate so many ups and downs in a day, week and month! My mind and body waxed and waned daily. Today was a good day, tomorrow not so much. Andee, said that I would have one good day and four not so hot days.

On May 27, 2008, I had significant facial swelling from the brain surgery. My family was frightened by my appearance. My temperature and blood pressure were elevating. On May 30, I opened my eyes once when orally suctioned and began to move both my legs and left arm for the first time. My fever persisted as well as the facial swelling. My mother, who is a registered nurse, told the nursing staff how concerned she was. Staff reported that brain swelling was common for many days following brain surgery. Dr. Ryken reported that I was progressing slowly, as he expected.

After not the first but the second surgery, the cranial bone flap was removed to allow my brain to swell, a necessity for healing. Around this time frame, Andee sensed that I had finally stabilized. Although unknown to anyone, this is the point when hard work truly begins. In the world of a traumatic brain injury patient, healing becomes more apparent when the patient begins following simple verbal commands consistently. Andee ranks a patient's status based on his/her ability to follow her official commands. She shares with families that having a traumatic brain injury patient resembles being on a roller coaster every single day! I was no different. Not only does this roller coaster occur in the intensive care unit but further onward, even through rehabilitation. Such reversions of the upside down roller coaster ride are emotionally taxing on both families and the nurses.

My youngest daughter Molly, age eight and in third grade, visited me for the first time following this second surgery! Molly was fearful and understood much less information than her siblings. Although this was May, Molly held my hand and sang "Silent Night," a song that Todd always sang to her. The words of the song that minister to me are "All is calm, all is bright...mother and child." Ryan, a soccer athlete and member of the Boy Scouts, had been to the hospital numerous times. He explained the accident to the entire fifth and sixth grade students. The school counselor said that his calmness in sharing his experience was remarkable.

When Meghan was an infant, Todd began to sing "Silent Night" to her at bedtime. Meghan first sang to us when she was only nine months old. She loves music and is gifted in singing. Her voice flourished while taking voice lessons. She succeeded to the degree that she became our family star as she sang to musical performances created by Meghan. She continued to venture further to sing solo in elementary and middle school performances, numerous musicals, and a wedding. The voice of Meghan was well known as many felt that she was a big hit! Within a month following my accident, Meghan auditioned for Show Choir at West High School which provides choir and dance. Unfortunately, she didn't achieve this dream of hers. Today, Meghan feels as if the physical and emotional trauma she was experiencing affected her true ability to sing. After witnessing me survive brain trauma above and beyond all expectations, Meghan made the show choir team for the last three years of high school. This illustrates the power of endurance achieved despite life's obstacles.

Todd would take the children to visit me after school, and return them home for bedtime. He would return to the hospital every night to visit me. On one school night, around ten p.m., Meghan, who was a freshman, asked if she could go with him back to the hospital. He told her "no", as she had school early the next day. She was furious and told him, "She's *my* mom and I should be allowed to see her whenever I want." Meghan explained how angry she felt about staying home and thus Todd agreed to take her with him. That night was the first time Meghan had ever seen her dad cry. She watched so many tears fall down his face. Standing in silence in the hospital room, Meghan also cried hoping so badly for me to awaken.

On June 2, 2008, nine days following my surgeries, I moved my mouth carefully around the endotracheal tube to tell my husband Todd, "I love you," somehow without the ability to verbalize anything out loud. He knew from my behavior what I was trying to say. I was tracking him with my eyes and feeling his face with my left hand. Meghan couldn't wait to hold my hand. When she visited that night, I actually opened my eyes without painful stimuli and looked around. Her spirit was enlightened. A dear friend Jenny was having a soft bracelet made for so many others to support me by wearing a wrist band. She asked Meghan what color she should use. Meghan stated "her favorite is purple." Jenny then asked for something that I say frequently to others, as she would put that on the other side of the bracelet. Meghan remarked, "Spread the love."

On some occasions, the only way that a patient responds is through some administration of pain. My right arm was not very active but my left hand was always searching for someone's hand. This new behavior was very encouraging to my family. I was not yet following commands, but I would nod in response to Todd's questions. I began moving my legs to the point where the nurses needed to secure them. When my legs were secured I moved them around quite a bit. I have loved music since I was very young. At the time when I began to move in the bed, my sister Kathleen smiled and played Salsa music which she knew I loved. Immediately my body and spirit mirrored the depth and dynamics of salsa music. I moved in and out of the initial position in the bed, kicking my legs harder and faster yet significantly to the beat. The incredible salsa music stimulated my brain's internal focus to move forward above and beyond being in a coma and restrained in my bed. Kathleen stopped the music for fear of damage to my IVs, ventilator tube, catheter, and feeding tube. Dad knew this was a real triumph as he followed my gradual recovery toward consciousness. It fostered the re-birth of such strength and stamina which was still in my spirit.

The beginning of summer, June 2008, carried the air of suspense, anticipation of threatening flood waters snaking their force into harm's way. Community volunteers rallied with drenched camaraderie. Mother Nature's fearlessness humbled all human dignities one sandbag at a time for hours and days. UIHC surgical intensive care unit safely cocooned a beautiful human being behind secured walls, monitoring severe brain trauma vital signs in a state of coma. Tangible sensations from family and friends witnessing a fragile life postured elements of what was happening on the outside world. Turbulent and eerie emotions striking the consciousness of where surrealism and suspense are at a stance with each other against a weighted heart. Outside and inside the walls of protected structure, grief pushed boundaries of discomforts mirroring the mysterious river's current…steadfast with tethered sorrow. The unknown of life's ebbs and flows.

The readiness to compassionately serve and be present by Bridgid's bedside was a 'call of duty' from a place beyond knowing her physical body from years of providing gentle, attentive chiropractic care. The presence of quietude after clinic hours led my heart to a place where I trusted Bridgid's body and soul could hear me…her subconscious mind knowing the skilled hands of trust hovering softly over her traumatized body and cranial bones protecting her brain under siege. A tiny movement of her hand indicated an energetic message after gently touching her skin with infusions of essential oils for tissue repair and cellular healing. Bridgid's physical body was in a coma, but her soul's code was on a journey that I fiercely understood from a near drowning "fight for life" in the unpredictable waters off the island of Maui in 2003. Several visits when bright lights were dimmed in her hospital room allowed moments of solace to whisper, "Bridgid, follow my voice, I know you can hear me, come back, come back...you have gifts to share...to teach others that will hear your voice. We all love you, Bridgid... come back, you have more healing work to do on earth in another way. Trust your heart, trust the voices of the angels to guide you."

—Dr. Jane Bourgeois

On June 3, I had an elevated fever, increased blood pressure of 160/90, a heart rate of 125, rapid breathing, and clear drainage fluid from my left ear. When my dad visited me that day he questioned the reason for the fluid drainage. My mother was convinced this was cerebral spinal fluid (CSF). The next day a physician sutured my left ear to reduce the drainage of the CSF. By June 5, I was much more drowsy than usual. Despite my symptoms, I was transferred from the SICU to an Intermediate Neuroscience Inpatient Unit. My white blood count increased to 34.8 (normal:

4.5–10.8) and hemoglobin decreased to 8.1 (normal: 12–16 gm/dL). A chest x-ray showed left lower lobe pneumonia. Antibiotics were provided. My mother noted even more swelling of the left side of my face and eye. The CSF continued to drain and I had 4 different nurses that particular morning! Inconsistency in progress and continuing changes within my system were hard for my family to witness.

On June 7, I had a vasovagal experience (a neurocardiogenic syncope which decreases the heart rate and blood pressure) when I was suctioned. I vomited and my heart rate dropped to the 50s and the T-wave abnormality on the EKG was notable. This could mean that the central nervous system was affected. I've noticed these neurocardiogenic symptoms when working with children who'd experienced similar trauma in the Pediatric ICU. The central nervous system is prone to abnormality following trauma. A medication was given to treat abnormal heart rhythms.

I still struggled with an off and on fever and was tested for a further infection. They tried to sit me in a supportive chair, but I was unable. My hematocrit and hemoglobin remained low, both of which indicate anemia. I was placed on iron to support red cell production. Antibiotics were adjusted for both pneumonia and a urinary tract infection. My family hoped my elevated temperature would normalize in response to the various antibiotics. When I did awaken, I could recognize people and sometimes nod yes or no to questions. I smiled and winked on occasion and was making a small neurological improvement. There was improved movement of my right arm and occasionally I would wave good-bye to visitors with my left hand. At times though, I was restless. Todd was informed that when I was medically stable and could stay awake for three hours, I would be transferred to a hospital that provided acute in-patient rehabilitation.

Andee came to visit me when I was placed into the neurological step-down unit. She smiled as she entered my room and saw my mother and sister Rachel near me. She asked how I was doing and what the plans were for me in regards to rehabilitation. My life experience was one day at a time and often one minute at a time. While Andee was visiting with them, they mentioned that it was time for me to be rotated in the bed. It is essential for bed rest patients to be turned every one to two hours to reduce the pressure within the pressure points of the body, as this enhances sufficient blood flow. They remarked that my nurse was so busy that day. Andee was so happy and honored that my family asked her to help them, as this was such a simple thing for her to do. Together they gently turned me over, washed my back, gave me some lip balm, and made great efforts to ensure that I was comfortable. Mom and Rachel were very appreciative that Andee took the time to care for me.

As Andee left my room that day, a tear fell down her face. She grieved for me, Todd and our children. By the time she returned to the ICU, her tears erupted. Her spirit wondered what life would be like if she were me in that hospital bed. Andee loves bicycle riding as I do and always wears a helmet. What on earth would it be like if it was her family having to explain to their children what had happened to their mother? The continuous question to Andee was, why? Why has this happened, as Andee felt that I did everything right! For months and months, Andee struggled and often questioned why life is so unfair! Not a day went by that Andee didn't think about me and wondered how I was doing. This type of behavior is very unlike Andee. She and other nurses try to emotionally distance themselves from patients, in an attempt to maintain their own sanity. Sure we all wonder how patients are doing, but I was a different type of patient to Andee.

On June 8, the cerebral spinal fluid continued draining and increased in the amount. Nurses thought that the water-filled cooling blanket may have ruptured. The blanket was beneath me to help to reduce my body temperature. There is a small probability that body pressure could have caused a rupture, but I was thin and continuing to lose weight. When I was examined, the cooling blanket was not damaged. Notice the swelling on the upper left side of my head, in the picture below. This demonstrates the continued swelling of my cerebral spinal fluid which kept draining beyond the normal time for it to cease. My heart rate, temperature, and blood pressure increased and I was becoming more and more lethargic. My brain was sending a message alerting others of my dangerous worsening symptoms.

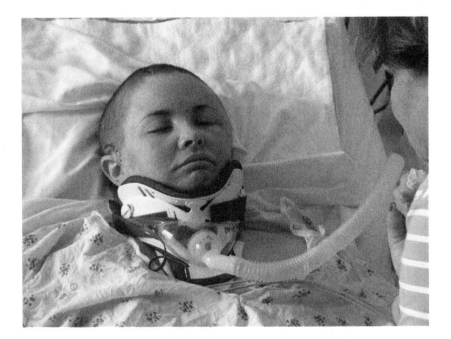

With much concern regarding the persistence of these symptoms, Todd shared his worries numerous times with a variety of health care staff. On a Sunday, he didn't receive a response or support for what he truly needed. He promptly worked his way upward from a medical student, to a resident and then asked to speak with a senior fellow neurosurgeon. This neurosurgeon listened and agreed with Todd's concerns. It is imperative that health care professionals pay attention to the loved one's concerns as they are directly involved with the patient many hours daily. Thank God the neurosurgeon respected Todd's concerns and ordered an MRI (Magnetic Resonance Imaging).

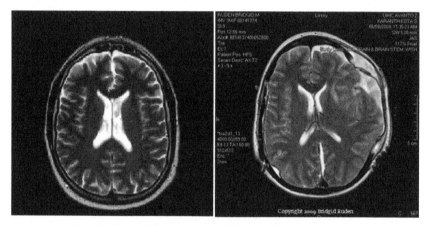

Normal Brain MRI   My MRI

The MRI indicated a potential increase in CSF, pus, and an infection within my brain. I needed an emergency surgery! Without emergent surgical treatment, a coma and death could occur rapidly. The bacterium was cultured. Infected area were cleaned and irrigated. I had one to two inches of my brain debrided from the abscess and a drain was placed in the subdural area. The abscess, the size of a small egg, was removed since it was seriously infected. I was transferred back to the ICU again! The next day I was returned to the neurology step-down unit following the removal of my staples and Hemovac, which suctions blood from a deep incision.

Despite these obstacles, I stabilized and exceeded everyone's expectations! Todd was amazed. I was the most alert that he had ever seen me. I opened my eyes independently. They were bright and I smiled more frequently. Intermittently I followed commands and simple directions. My body temperature was low grade. My family was informed that further progress would be slow and there could be more setbacks. They were cautiously optimistic.

Todd began to share updates on my condition through a free website called (www.carepages.com). Care Page provides a valuable way to communicate life changing health experiences with others. This provides families and friends a support circle. You document the patient's progress and an outlet for friends to respond as well. My Care Page reached thousands of people. My friend and colleague, Susie Green, had a hard time believing in the seriousness of the accident until Todd shared the situations, and she was able to grasp the severity knowing what was at stake and that I was fighting for my own life. Susie and so many others valued the ability to view Care Page since they were able to stay up-to-date on my development .

I was placed on numerous prayer chains. Prayers occurred above and beyond anything that I have even imagined. Many of the prayer groups even involved religious organizations outside the United States. My dad stated that many individuals we have never known prayed for our family, and those prayers continue to this day. Dad is asked weekly by so many people wondering about my condition today. My precious father-in-law, Dick, calls once a week asking how I'm doing. He prays for me every day.

Prayers to the Divine demonstrate a very powerful way miracles arise. We all have such gratitude for the prayers and support provided to me and our family. Todd's mother, Norene, felt the praying beat a path to heaven and pleaded with God to heal me. She strongly believes that all the prayers for my recovery created a miracle. Mom wrote on the Care Page what I would say to all praying, "Thank you and spread the love."

When my life returned, I was propelled backwards in time from forty-four years of age to three years of age. I relearned so many life skills. On June 12, I was in less pain and stood up with assistance from two people. This was my first experience standing since the accident. My legs were very weak, but daily my strength was increasing. On June 13, I was able to move my legs and shuffle across the floor with significant support. Later, I was able to sit in a chair with my helmet on for seventy-five amazing minutes! I was more aware of my surroundings.

I had a decreased ability to get my tongue out of my mouth. This was a result of my tracheotomy and loss of air to the vocal chords. Despite this, I occasionally tried to mouth a word. I somehow tried to ask why I was here. What was the cause of my accident? I wanted so much more information. No memory of what was told to me ever appeared. Each day Todd noticed progress. It might have been small to others but I continued to move forward. I could stick out my tongue and more clearly mouth a word on an occasion. At one point I clearly mouthed, "I want to go home." I was able to walk forty feet very slowly with a physical therapist. The kids were very impressed with my progress. Molly surprised me with her artwork. I winked at her and she smiled at me! Over the next few days, I made remarkable steps forward to a surprising recovery.

Rehabilitation was now considered. Health care staff assumed I would be transferred to On With Life Rehabilitation Hospital in Des Moines, Iowa. This would be two hours from our home. Todd knew in his heart that I would be very displeased to be so far away from home. The only way I could be thirty minutes from Coralville would be a newer rehabilitation program at St. Luke's Hospital in Cedar Rapids, Iowa. University of Iowa physicians were not comfortable with this admission with my tracheotomy tube still in place. Todd so wished for the tracheotomy to be removed as he knew what my response would be when my memory returned. Miraculously, Todd's prayer was answered. As the trach was disconnected, I began to breathe effectively and voiced my first words in three weeks! I softly said, "Thank you," as if my spirit knew of such triumph. My voice was soft. But it was so fantastic for everyone to truly hear me speak.

CHAPTER 6

Life's Roller Coaster

My first partial return of my memory occurred when I was placed on an ambulance cart at the University of Iowa. I briefly remember smiling and waving goodbye to the nurse's aide who assisted me. I don't recall getting into the ambulance to drive to St. Luke's Hospital, but I do recall being in the ambulance and wondering where on earth was I? I could hear the sounds of the vehicle driving. Where was I going? What was I lying on and why was no one talking to me? Flooding had significantly occurred in Iowa City, Cedar Rapids, and central Iowa; therefore, the trip was lengthy. When I arrived at St. Luke's, my memory came and went. No matter how hard we try to resolve this, short term memory is the most lasting effect of traumatic brain injury. My precious mother stayed with me every night in a bed next to me. It was reassuring that Dad's cousin, Barb Kluesner, RN, was the rehabilitation nursing care-manager as she was such a support person for Mom and me. I was so thin—114 pounds. Mom asked for pediatric pajamas as the adult size barely stayed on. I started physical, recreational, speech and occupational therapy. I was very tired, but glad to begin recovery.

My language consisted of speaking a few words at a time and was difficult for others to understand as I often didn't say the correct word. I, like so many brain injury survivors, have aphasia. Aphasia is the loss of the ability to produce or comprehend language, secondary to damage in the brain area associated with these functions. This creates a barrier in the ability to communicate verbally or use written words. For example, I love sleeping with a fan. One evening, I looked at mom and said, "an electric flower." Amazingly, Mom knew I meant to say "fan." How powerful mothers are in recognizing their child's needs. I struggled finding the right words and often did not understand a question.

Molly loves horses and is an English horseback rider. I saw a picture of a horse and smiled. I knew in my brain what the picture was but I could not say the word "horse." This saddened me. I wanted so badly to say the name of Molly's favorite animal. Molly began riding lessons at eight years old, prior to my accident. Molly was in heaven when she and her horse friends stayed in a stall overnight, in anticipation of a mare delivering a colt. Unfortunately, during the time I was unable to drive, I could no longer take Molly to her horse riding lessons. In my mind's eye, this was tragic for her as she stopped taking riding lessons for quite a while.

On June 18, I had sixty-two staples and one suture removed from my head! Wearing a helmet was mandatory since I had no skull on my left side. Meghan and Molly decorated my helmet with beautifully colored flowers, hearts, and several sunshines. Flowers, hearts, and sunshine have always been very dear to my spirit. Their combination of art work is so very healing. "Mom" is written on both the front and back of the helmet. Three days later I rode on a wheelchair outside with a physical therapist. After being indoors for so long, being outdoors was a powerful experience for me. Witnessing and being a part of a beautiful, sunny day and a flower garden was divine.

One morning I even got up and went to the bathroom by myself, which I wasn't supposed to do. Shocker! I tend to do whatever I feel capable of doing regardless of the unknown consequences. My mother noted my progress in recovery every day. It was slow but steady, not as fast as I personally wanted to proceed. Mom explains to me the process it took to help "rebirth her daughter." Mom feels our path together was so meaningful and integrated. People couldn't believe the manner in which I promptly accelerated after three brain surgeries.

My friend Susie recalls what she saw the first time she visited me in rehabilitation. As she walked into the room she witnessed me lying curled up in the hospital bed in a fetal-like position. She could tell from my demeanor that my head was hurting. Susie could also tell that my mom was truly present to protect me. She didn't know if I would remember her. Even though I was not using my voice, I reached out my hand toward her and held it, as if I truly knew who she was. Susie was still shocked at seeing me without hair or skull and in significant pain. Despite this, Susie still felt hope. Such a beautiful symbol for Susie to see as it guided her belief in me. I had begun to speak and put several words together for the first time when Susie had come to visit me. Naturally, my speech was not very clear. To Susie it sounded garbled or mushy, but it was still understandable with my mom's help.

A week later, Susie asked my mom if she could come to visit again. Mom allowed people to come for only short visits, which was so necessary. I had just slowly relearned how to eat again. My gastrointestinal tube, which I needed for long-term nutrition, was temporarily closed to determine if my stomach supported eating food by mouth. I smiled as Susie brought broccoli cheese soup, my ultimate favorite. Recalling how I appeared a week earlier, Susie had prepared herself to witness the same scene. I was vastly different—sitting up and starting to speak, a completely different person. I spoke so much more clearly than the week before. Susie was still experiencing shock. But this time her hope for my continued healing was even stronger, as she witnessed true miracles occurring in me.

Being outside within all aspects of nature is a powerful way to minister to my soul. I remember feeling so frustrated and isolated having to remain inside during my hospitalizations. When I was able to walk outside for the first time I felt naturally high! I required a gait belt for stability. My physical therapist accompanied me on my walk and held on to my gait belt. To truly visualize green grass and the warm temperature was stunning. Flowers blossomed into various beautiful rainbow colors which mesmerized me. My heart was so uplifted, my soul so exhilarated that being present in nature provided such a powerful way to guide me in my healing process. I craved continuing to stay right there in that environment of blessings.

But I did have an unpleasant experience with an occupational therapist. She walked with me and I had to go across a one-way street. I looked but didn't see a car coming so I started to go across. She stated that I was supposed to look twice, as this could be a busy street. Assuming that I was not yet knowledgeable about safety and perhaps had impaired judgment, she stated that I would never go directly home after discharge. I would instead be placed in a nursing home. What? I am a mother of three children. How could I care for them away from home, living where disabled elderly live! In addition, she stated that it would take me so very long to re-learn how to drive. I felt as if I had failed. Anger, sadness, and fear merged and rolled through my system. What do you think I would do in a nursing home? Yes, I'd rapidly focus on my healing, but I would also strive to help other patients who were suffering. My spirit of determination emerged even stronger as I thought, "I'm going to show you!"

One of my goals was learning how to eat. On June 23, I had a test to determine my ability to swallow foods. Passing this test was a fabulous experience. I was so grateful that the gastric feeding tube stopped feeding me, but the tube itself stayed in case there were problems. I actually ate a real meal with Todd and my daughter Meghan in the rehab dining room! On June 24, I was ready to take oral medication and eat breakfast, and my appetite was slowly improving.

On another incredible day, Mom could not believe the difference she noticed for the very first time. I had an engaging conversation with her. Sometimes I was slightly confused or at a loss for words, but Mom felt I was moving forward! One day, when I wasn't feeling so well, I wrote the names of Meghan, Ryan and Molly for the first time despite the poor strength in my left arm. I also shockingly gave Todd a phone message that the oil needed to be changed in the van and to schedule this for Friday! Unbelievably, I somehow knew my parents would be using our van to drive to Jackson Hole, Wyoming with our children for my brother's wedding. The van had 4,500 miles since the last oil change. Mom has saved this phone message. Mom states that my progress is proof that God hears and answers our prayers.

My brother Peter came to visit me despite the fact that he rarely traveled to Iowa. I was thrilled when he arrived. Peter has always made me laugh so hysterically. His name was identified as "Pistol Packing Peter." Peter and his fiancée Mimi were going to be married in Jackson Hole, Wyoming, in one month. Physicians wouldn't let me get on a plane to go to his wedding since part of my skull was missing. I was so angry and really tried to change Todd's and their minds. Being the oldest of eight has been an incredibly rewarding opportunity in my life. I always want to be present for each sibling as I'm needed. I had forgotten what I was doing for Peter and Mimi prior to my accident. Kathleen informed me that I had nearly finished a musical video to surprise Peter and Mimi. The video to be shown at the wedding reception was created to share pictures of them from birth toward the time they drew together. Thank God, Kathleen knew and shared this video at their reception. As Peter was leaving the hospital, he threw his arms around me and softly said, "I love you, Bridgid," as tiny tears dripped from his eyes. I was astonished as "I love you" was something I had never heard Peter say before. A divine healer was providing continued miracles in my pathway!

By July 3, 2008, I was still on track to be discharged. Oh yes, home I was headed! Everyone was very excited about bringing me home! The day before, we had a family conference which consisted of meeting with the Physical Therapist (PT), Speech Therapist (ST), Occupational Therapist (OT), Rehabilitation Nurse Coordinator, Social Worker, and Psychologist. Thank God, a team approach! Each one discussed how well I was progressing but outlined certain limitations for my safety. These limitations were not necessarily permanent.

A very concerning problem occurred when the physician who supported my discharge smiled and said, "Bye-bye, Bridgid, good luck!" He never offered nor suggested continuous follow-up medical care! Unfortunately, this occurs frequently when persons with brain injury are being discharged from inpatient rehabilitation. Guess what? This is a lifelong disease! Todd was infuriated and called the University of Iowa to establish continued physical, occupational, speech, cognitive, and psychological care from a physician trained in working with brain injury survivors.

Physical therapists (PT) felt that I was doing wonderfully. They had never witnessed a patient relearn to walk and be discharged wanting to sprint again! Unfortunately, they gave me an odd look and didn't allow me to do this. Towards the end of my hospital rehabilitation, I attempted to walk as fast as I could on a treadmill, wishing so badly that I could gently jog again. Physical therapists were shocked by my determination. No, they did not allow me to jog even gently. My "lovely" brain helmet that I didn't feel comfortable wearing needed to be worn at all times when I was out of bed due to the fact that my left bone flap was still missing. Yes, I often forgot to put on this ridiculous thing. I needed someone around 24-7 for safety concerns. I was not allowed to go up or down stairs by myself. I also needed to continue to wear a Miami cervical collar for neck support since I had fractured my cervical 6 vertebrae. I met a PT only twice a week and asked to resume learning to swim despite my balance issues and broken right clavicle. Once I learned how to swim again despite right clavicle pain, I completed physical therapy! Well, I thought physical therapy was dismissed in my journey.

Speech therapists felt that I had made good progress in the last three weeks and had a lot better understanding of what I was reading or trying to say. I didn't always recognize mistakes, but I was becoming more aware of this. For reading, I was beginning to recognize words, but I still couldn't always remember the meaning. For writing, I could write the word "okay" but often misspelled.

I was doing a great job swallowing and gently eating; therefore I did not have to re-use my stomach tube at all! Yeah! A gastric feeding tube (G-tube or "button") is a tube inserted through a small incision in the abdomen into the stomach. A feeding tube is a medical device used to provide nutrition to patients who cannot obtain nutrition by mouth, are unable to swallow safely, or need nutritional supplementation. Although I didn't need to use the tube, St. Luke's wasn't ready to let it go. No, I was not happy about this as I wanted this G-tube out now!

Occupational therapists (OT) felt that I had come a long way in three weeks. I was shocked and wondered if all of them truly felt that way. One particular occupational therapist stated how very long it would take me to re-learn how to drive again, the same OT who thought I would be going to a nursing home. No one else on the health care team ever mentioned this or the possibility of being discharged to a nursing home. I continued to proceed with determination knowing that I was going to prove her wrong! I had high expectations of myself. Many noted my spunk and determination to drive and how this propelled me forward.

A psychologist told me that my language impairment sometimes makes cognitive testing look worse than it may really be. I had issues with organizing and planning which is called Executive Dysfunction. Therefore, one requirement was that I receive help with planning my own daily schedule first and then the family's needs. I couldn't be the same busy mom I had been prior to my accident. The health care team stated that my number one job was to focus on my recovery, no one else. I frowned, since it wasn't a piece of cake for a mother who previously gave 200 percent for our family. My vision for my future also included returning to the University of Iowa Hospital and resuming my position as a pediatric nurse practitioner. I shared something like this with the team and they shook they heads and stated, "Not now." More was to be revealed to me about this later in my journey.

CHAPTER 7

Being a Pistol

Once I was finally home, after a short nap, Mom and I walked outside to explore the backyard and our large oak tree which shattered. There had been a great deal of rain and thus the ground became soft and didn't provide support for the tree. Seeing my flowers was such a huge delight. I love and appreciate nature so much! I kneeled down on the soft ground and began weeding around my flowers. Dad looked at me and shook his head "no", as if he was thinking I was doing too much. I thought I needed to nurture my flowers, to accomplish something that brought light to my spirit. Although I needed 24-7 supervision due to safety concerns, I was nicknamed Houdini Because of my tendency to "disappear." I could walk slowly, but occasionally I'd become lightheaded and dizzy because of my balance issues. Do you think that stopped me? That first morning when I was home, I got up without waking Todd. I proceeded to feed the cat (Angel) and dog (Petey). I knew that Petey needed to go outside to do his business so I followed him. Petey got loose and ran to the neighbor's house. I walked as fast as I could and managed to get him despite beginning to get light-headed. As dangerous as this is, I forgot to wear my helmet! Todd was not thrilled with my behavior.

I could get dressed on my own but with supervision. Yes, I seemed to need supervision frequently with bathing, medication and money matters. Do you think I followed that rule? I was not allowed to cook for safety reasons. My youngest, Molly, at age eight, taught me how to use a microwave once I was home. I was able to prove that I could do some laundry, which enlightened my spirit to be a part of the team. Everyone eventually learned the necessity of a daily nap for me. Exhaustion, confusion and sometimes tears begin to appear five hours after I've awaken. The tears may surface because I feel so badly that I can't complete much in a day as I did previously. I need two to three hours of sleep. I've noted that when I require a three-hour nap, I have done way too much.

But I have always been independent, and I wasn't going to sit around and take it as health care providers and my family wanted me to do. Todd was shocked when I started to multitask so promptly after returning home. I was sitting on the floor, reorganizing clothes for each child and placing them in dressers but did this while talking to Meghan on a phone. I kept the phone together and kept a wedge between my helmet and Miami neck brace. Finally, in the middle of July, I was thrilled to have my gastrointestinal tube and Miami neck brace removed.

Several weeks after returning home, I had a 3D CT scan to determine the safety of having my bone flap replacement. The neurosurgeon said that my bone flap would need to be replaced with a titanium flap, due to microorganisms on the original flap. He was initially hesitant about replacing the bone flap too early due to the previous infection, *Enterobacter cloaca.* After discussing with infectious disease physicians, they acquired a target date of the first week of August for the bone flap replacement surgery. I asked him to not remove the tiny amount of hair that had re-grown over my scalp. The re-growth of my hair in a way represented my own growth in recovery and I didn't want it taken away. He thought about it and said, "Well, okay." I was thrilled as I had some control over something.

Todd was amazed that I improved weekly and that my memory was gradually improving. I was able to remember what occurred two days before my accident but not any about the accident itself. My strength was improving, although I tired so easily. When the Miami cervical collar was removed, I developed constant vertigo. I thought I had departed permanently from physical therapists but I was wrong. I have such admiration for all the care they provide patients. St. Luke's Physical Therapist (PT) thought the vertigo may be due to debris which can collect within a part of the inner ear after a head injury. This is caused when infection or inflammation stop the tiny calcium "stones" inside the inner ear from moving as they should. This sends a false message to the brain and affects a person's balance. This can also cause: dizziness, lightheadedness, visual changes, swaying, lack of balance, feeling faint and nausea. When vertigo occurred, my vision was poor and I could not walk effectively. Medications given in the ER were never effective for me.

Physical therapists used an incredible technique called the Epley and Semont Maneuver. When my head was firmly moved into different positions, it would then slip out of the semicircular canal into an area of the inner ear where it would no longer cause symptoms. When they completed this procedure, I stood and walked normally and could see perfectly! This can be provided at home but I forgot what all to do and Todd had been through enough. Besides, I loved seeing these wonderful healing PTs again.

When years later I was in Florida, I decided to kayak on a beautiful day with wonderful weather and waves that were softly displaying their realm of movement. Kayaking is a peaceful nurturing experience. I ventured forth alone as no one was around that area of the ocean. I never thought about the potential of a nasty seizure occurring during my isolation from others. I felt the waves were simple and didn't even think about the possibility of vertigo. Todd later took me for a drive for dinner and had to turn sharply which caused my head and neck to hit the window. This only hurt minimally thus I let that experience mist away. The next morning I went to the shower and started to fall several times with intense dizziness. I had no idea what was occurring. I then became so nauseated and could barely walk. I walked to reach my computer and couldn't visualize the words from the typing I had done. This was definitely the worst vertigo I had ever had.

I called the ER to ask if they had a physical therapist that worked with those with vertigo. The nurse stated that I should head to the ER as soon as possible. I felt differently. Amazing Todd found a qualified physical therapist with his own business. I was thrilled to meet another healing physical therapist. Not only did he use the Epley and Semont maneuvers but also provided Electrotherapeutic Point Stimulation (ETPS)—electrical stimulation used to treat acupuncture points. This decreases any abnormal muscle tone in the eye, as well as any pain and nausea. Primal Reflex Release (PRRT) is used for relaxation and has dramatic effects on the nervous system. Relaxation occurred immediately! After these 3 treatments: I could walk again, wasn't nauseated or feeling so down & worried! I felt utter JOY! Physical therapists who work with brain injury survivors should value the healing impacts of these incredible techniques. They are used throughout the world! Therefore, true healing can occur well beyond medication!

On July 17, I had a follow-up appointment with the neurosurgeon, Dr. Tim Ryken, at the University of Iowa Hospitals and Clinics. The purpose of the appointment was to inspect my head wound and verify there was no infection in preparation of the August 5 titanium bone flap replacement surgery. They also drew blood to get baseline measurements before the surgery. We asked about the weakness in my left grip strength and mentioned that the vision in my left eye was not as it was prior to the accident. The weakness could be caused by some nerve damage due to the fall. Dr. Ryken examined the CT scan from the week earlier and compared it to earlier scans. The CT still showed areas of bruising on the left side of the brain. As I was still healing, it was a waiting game to see how the hand strength improved with Occupation Therapy (OT). Dr. Ryken recommended that I see a neuro-ophthalmologist to assess my vision. Overall, Dr Ryken was impressed with my recovery process and I was scheduled for a preoperational physical on August 4. After the surgery on August 5, he felt that I would be in the SICU for a day and then to a step-down unit for about two days.

Until that time, I continued with PT, OT, and Speech Therapy three times a week, usually in the morning. After about three hours of intense work, I was exhausted. I napped about three hours in the afternoon and was in bed by eight. Sleep disorders are three times more common in traumatic brain injury survivors than the general public. Sixty percent of survivors have long-term sleep disorders, which are more likely to occur in women.

In the morning, my shoulders were sore and neck was stiff. Massage therapy was a necessity which I continually do once a month. The kids were great about rubbing my feet, helping with my homework, teaching me how to use kitchen cooking materials and assisting me around the house. My children were caregivers aiding me in healing! My homework consisted of stretching, strengthening and balancing exercises, hand exercises with putty, and picture and word identification.

On August 5, 2008, I had my final brain surgery, a titanium bone flap replacement surgery, because my left bone flap was found to be contaminated with bacteria (anaerobic strep) and thus was sent to the garbage. Despite having part of my left skull gone, the picture below displays a glorious smile depicting the love, grace, and connectedness I have with my beautiful mother.

I was excited that my naked skull was going to be re-filled with a titanium skull soon. Another wish came true as the surgeon listened to my request and didn't shave off my hair again! My precious sister Rachel stayed with me overnight during my hospitalization! Rachel watched over me like a hawk and ministered tremendous guidance, love and support.

Pain is generally enhanced in brain injury survivors compared to others without the same brain trauma. Rachel and I were very displeased when a neurosurgical resident removed the brain's blood drainage tube without adequately preparing me for what was about to happen. This is a very painful procedure. Before the removal of the tube, the resident barely spoke to me, showed no compassion or understanding, and no remorse for the pain I experienced. It is essential to communicate gently and provide simple information to any patient. Be honest about the upcoming process and support one's experience.

Anyone serving others who are struggling internally from challenges in their own life is at risk to release their pain outside of themselves, which then impacts those around you. Today, I question what was occurring in her life? Perhaps a stressful job, lack of sufficient sleep, troubled home life, health issues, or any other tragedies in her life that may need addressing? One of the essential keys of being a healer is to put aside your own present life experiences when caring for someone. Without letting go of your present struggles, this is effortlessly transferred forward to the person needing healing. This is best accomplished by taking care of your own emotional, mental and physical necessities first. The best healer embraces this and can easily focus and honor messages that any survivor's mind, body, and spirit sends. Therefore, true healing for any survivor ascends when the health care provider focuses on his/her own self-care first.

CHAPTER 8

Miracles and Mishaps

As the big wigs were preparing to discharge me following this latest surgery, Todd worried about establishing suitable homecare for our family. I was not capable of being left alone at all. Of course, I denied this. Todd was so grateful that my aunt Katie arrived from Los Angeles, California to help care for me and the children.

Katie shared how rewarding her experience was going to so many appointments to hear therapists and physicians share their astonishment at my progress which moved beyond expectations. Katie loved it that I was "kicking butt" with great tenacity and spirit, which is pretty common for me. I was moved to tears daily from the encouragement I received and asked Katie to spread my love and gratitude to everyone saying prayers and keeping me close in their hearts. I am a grateful receiver. The amount of love shown to me is so very powerful. I witnessed this when reading the numerous messages I received on Care Page. I have been told that I am loved by so many.

Before discharge, Dr. Ryken was impressed with my recovery. I no longer had any physical limitations other than my right shoulder being tender from the broken clavicle. He wanted me to take it slow. Once when Mom and I visited, I wanted to know whether I was really making progress as I did not see this myself. Naturally, I was pretty hard on myself and wished my true recovery would go faster. Mom often reminded me how shocked the medical community was regarding the tremendous speed of my recovery. What seemed like small steps really did add up. My mom saw that the support, love, and prayers from everyone had a lot to do with my determination and tenacity and have made an incredible difference in my progress.

I laid down one day on a hammock at my parent's backyard. I loved swaying back and forth on a warm beautiful summer day. Molly tried to join me. Once she laid on me, the pressure tossed me off the hammock and onto the right side of my head. I developed vertigo but had no desire to head to an emergency room. A physical therapist wasn't available to provide me with the Epley and Semont maneuver. My friend who is a chiropractor insisted that I go to the ER. Begrudgingly I went. I was excited when a wonderful woman who took the CT scan asked if I'd like to view my titanium plate. My mouth hung open and I stood in shock as I realized that I truly did have a fake skull. Below are CTs that demonstrate the look of my titanium plate on the left and the fracture on the right side of my skull. I found this very fascinating to observe my titanium plate. Thank you God there was no damage from my fall.

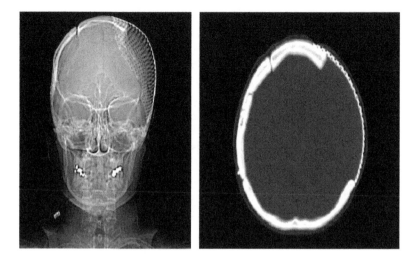

By October, I continued to make slow and steady progress in outpatient rehabilitation. My therapists told me that rehabilitation is a full time job now. I completed a three and a half hour cognitive test from Dr. Robert Jones, a neuropsychologist from the University of Iowa Hospitals and Clinics. The test results showed that I had anomia (a type of aphasia characterized by problems recalling words or names). Sometimes I could recall a word when given clues. My reading and writing ability were progressing slowly but the auditory comprehension and memory were much improved.

I wondered when I would be able to return to my position as a pediatric nurse practitioner at the University of Iowa Hospital. When I asked Dr. Jones, he looked at me very seriously and stated, "Bridgid, 90 percent of folks with traumatic brain injury can't go back to their previous job." He was trying to shoot straight with me, as he explained that I no longer had my previous medical knowledge. In addition, my aphasia would create barriers in effectively communicating with patients, their family and colleagues. Unfortunately, he was not the only physician who devastated my spirit. I was in utter denial, shocked, sad, angry and bewildered. Why me? In my inner spirit, I wanted to "show them," I was determined to return to my position as a pediatric nurse practitioner in Neonatology.

I was given an UFOV (Useful Field of View) test for driving. Thank God I scored in the highest category (low risk). I then took the original license test and failed. I was so saddened. A friend who is a stroke survivor, drove me to the DOT stated, "Bridgid, you are disabled. They must know that." For the second time, with shame I told them my disabilities. They then provided me with oral testing where they would read to me and I could point to the picture. My heart flourished as I passed the first time! Later, I truly succeeded in mastering an "over the road" Department of Transportation (DOT) test! Finally, I could drive again which was especially important as a mother of three children. I loved this new freedom to be able to drive again and not ask nor burden anyone for rides.

CHAPTER 9

Epilepsy Unfolds

Based on both my training and experience as a pediatric nurse and expertise within my own family, I was knowledgeable about the dynamic of various types of seizures, their impacts and treatment strategies. Molly had been a very healthy baby. Yet at six months of age, she spontaneously developed myoclonic epilepsy. My brother Glen and sister-in-law Karin noticed the first episode. They shared with me that Molly occasionally had very brief muscle spasms in her upper body. I had been keeping my eyes open to detect these myself. Days later, Molly was sitting in a booster chair eating when her head dropped forward in a jerking fashion for a few seconds and frequently reoccurred. She was awake and coherent as a six-month-old typically is. My mother's sixth sense emerged and I took her immediately to the emergency room. With the testing they determined that Molly was seizing. She was hospitalized for one week in an attempt to control the seizures. She received continuous EEG (electroencephalograph) to provide concrete evidence of the electrical activity in the brain. An EEG can help determine the type of seizure present.

Myoclonic seizures can occur as early as infancy. "Myo" is defined as muscle and "clonus" means jolting of a muscle. Routinely they last one to two seconds, although sometimes several will occur in a short period of time. These seizures may be difficult to notice as they are short and correlate as typical movement. This is how her seizures were displayed and they increased to thirty-five to forty-five per day. Yes, I was frightened, as I was well aware of potential diagnosis, such as West Syndrome. The seizure is described as infantile spasms which don't necessarily have a very good prognosis neurologically. I had worked previously with children with West Syndrome. The myoclonic presentation of the seizures that occur are the same as Molly's. Many children develop other kinds of epilepsy and became developmentally and cognitively delayed. My colleague was Molly's pediatric neurologist. I shared my fear with her. She looked at me seriously and said, "Bridgid, don't go there automatically, let's see how this treatment works."

I needed to focus my attention on the fact that all testing came back negative. My fears were lessened as her seizures reduced when placed on an anticonvulsant, a "valium" like derivative, and high-dose steroids. Her cognitive development continued at a normal pace. The last time she had a myoclonic seizure was at nine months of age. Certain types of seizures have the potential to return around five years of age and during adolescence. Although we were uncertain of her developmental future—she never ceases to amaze us! She was talking in sentences at eighteen months and can get into more mischief than the older two combined. Molly is now an adolescent and, thus far, her seizures have not returned. So many prayers given to Molly guided her in healing.

She fractured her wrist as a toddler in daycare when she ran to greet me and fell. In less than a month's time frame, she removed two casts and a splint when I wasn't around her!! She smiled and said, "See, Mom, all better now!" Molly was begging me to place her in kindergarten when she just turned four! When she was young she dreamed of being a "kitty doctor" someday. She cracked me up when hearing a new male pediatrician call her a "princess" during a health care exam. Molly remarked she didn't like him calling her a "princess." She gave me an angered look, "Mom, when he calls me that I want to cough up a hair ball!" Molly is very social, driven, and fiercely independent, something that has flourished even more since my accident. Recently, Molly shared that her true independence emerged following my accident, as she was "raising herself" at that time. This thoroughly breaks my heart and places such shame within me.

There is a potential that seizures will occur following traumatic brain injury. In November 2008, neurologists felt it was safe for me to stop my seizure medication. I was thrilled! I wanted to be off as much medication as I could be. In January 2009, I had a natural high as I began to drive again! My spirit was thrilled as I could return driving my children to wherever they needed to be. I loved the fact that I could begin to resume some of my responsibilities as their mother.

But with my memory loss, I accidently drove thirty miles to Cedar Rapids instead of Iowa City for Ryan's soccer game, the sport he loved so very much. Oops! Instead of seeing Ryan's game, I headed to shop with Meghan in Cedar Rapids. She was ecstatic to finally have special time with her mom! A further triumph occurred afterward when I drove to get our family groceries. This was a huge success. I had never completed so many activities in one day. I was so proud to reestablish my previous motherhood style. Unfortunately, I learned another life lesson. I was doing way too much work for our family. Fatigue occurs within me in five to six hours after awakening. I'd forgotten that I require a two-three hour nap daily, a necessity and priority in healing from TBI.

While I was putting away the groceries, my mother called. Distracted, confused speech erupted through my voice. I was barely able to use words effectively. My mother, an incredible nurse, feared that I was going to have a seizure. She talked to my son Ryan and then heard a loud crash. At twelve years of age, Ryan witnessed a reflection of me in the window falling face first onto the hardwood floor in the kitchen. My body was in complete spasm and I was bleeding from my mouth and nose. I was experiencing a grand mal seizure, a sudden attack or convulsion with muscle spasm and loss of consciousness. Ryan called 911 and turned me to my side and pinched my nose so that I could breathe! The police officer who was present was amazed at how calm Ryan was in providing emergency care to his own mother at twelve years of age! Ryan is my hero.

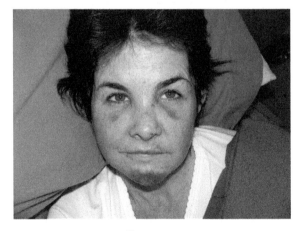

Appearance Following My First Seizure

When looking back in time, I was reminded that Ryan at four years of age called 911. He wanted to "talk to a policeman" and discussed the emergency that our "computer was broken." Even though he was terrified, Ryan had an appropriate talk with the police officer and better understood emergency. Ryan knew to call 911 when I was unconscious. When Ryan was in kindergarten, we found a small injured kitten bleeding from his mouth and nose. Ryan held that kitten so gently in a blanket while I drove to a pet clinic. Ryan asked, "Mom, am I doing a good job taking care of this little kitty?" When Ryan was eight and in second grade, he enthusiastically started Cub Scouts and mentioned that he envisioned becoming a scientist someday.

In high school, one of Ryan's favorite classes is Science. The word science comes from the Latin word *scientia*, "knowledge." The dictionary defines science as: "The intellectual and practical activity encompassing the systematic study of the structure and behavior of the physical and natural world through observation and experience." With Ryan's incredible background, who knows where the path will lead him in life's journey.

In recognition of all that Ryan did for me at twelve years of age, he has received a National Medal of Merit from the Boy Scouts and the American Legion, Iowa's Life Saving Award, and Hero of the Year award from the Brain Injury Association of Iowa.

Post-traumatic epilepsy has a high propensity to occur when one experiences 1) a prolonged loss of consciousness, 2) memory loss of trauma experienced, 3) skull fracture, or 4) bleeding of the skull or within the brain. I had all four of these. Yes, I was returned to seizure medication. My driver's license was revoked for six months each time I had a grand-mal seizure. This continued over a two year time period!

One day, a woman named Mary Thompson, a Reiki therapist, visited with me before providing me with Reiki, an ancient Japanese tradition which promotes healing. That day, a great deal of stress had occurred based on incidents that I couldn't control. So much of life we can't control, though I've wanted to do so. I was trying to share this with Mary but lost my ability to speak efficiently. An odd feeling occurred within my chest. Mary laid me down on a comfortable table to rest, but unfortunately I began to seize and thus became unconscious. An unusual experience emerged within me, something that I would call "out of body." I began to hear the sound of myself seizing. My mind recalled hearing such a gurgling sound, as one I had heard before from seizing patients for whom I provided care. In addition, I could feel my muscle rigidity and convulsion.

Despite being unconscious, I could feel Mary's loving hand wipe the saliva from my face and the sound of her gentle, loving voice reassuring me. I awoke slowly, confused and in and out of responsiveness. To me, I felt this was an out of body experience, which provided me with further understanding of the aspects of a grand-mal seizure in action. After this experience, I began to pay alert attention to both my decreased ability to speak effectively, anxiety, and the odd sensation I felt in my chest, as these occurred directly before the seizure. Although it is difficult for those with epilepsy to explain the physiological impact of an aura, it symbolizes a particular bodily sensation communicating that a seizure is nearly upon you. Personal encounters of auras documented in the WebMD website, include a visual change such as bright lights, strange size and shape of objects, zigzag lines, spots which spread slowly, and dark spots. Other indicators include hearing voices or sounds, odd smells, numbness or tingling on one side of the face or body, out of body sensation, anxiety, or nausea. My aura delivers a sensation within the center of my chest. If an aura is displayed within my system, this indicates my need to reduce my anxiety. The brain's neuron cells which provide me with an aura, is a reminder for me to ingest my anti-anxiety medication which I take under my tongue. I often forget to take the medicine. Today my brain is beginning to emphasize my needed direction so much more often.

Epilepsy shuffled and altered my mind and spirit. I never wanted seizures to return. But once again, so much of life is out of my control. At this point, denial of the epilepsy diagnosis sounded good to me. My precious mother had an incredible medical alert bracelet made for me. On one side is caduceus, the medical symbol. On the other side is written epilepsy, the name of my medication, and Todd's phone number. Attached was a heart-shaped piece that stated my name and my accreditation as a pediatric nurse practitioner. This brought such tears to my eyes. I listened to my mother and wore the bracelet, though I've learned that many with epilepsy don't. Medical bracelets are crucial to educate others who are with you in any critical situation.

Lo and behold, I discovered that there was a monthly epilepsy support group in Iowa City. The value of connecting with those who have the same disease or other causalities is remarkable. This provides an incredible opportunity to enhance your knowledge base and be surrounded with such validation, support, hope and strategies towards healing. I heard folks talk about other types of seizures, and my eyes rushed open in amazement. They discussed preseizure symptoms of another type of seizure, which I experienced. I learned by listening as reading books was too challenging. When I shared my experience, group members mentioned that I had symptoms of simple partial seizures. When these occur, I am fully conscious with unusual sensations that last for several minutes. Often, I start gagging and can't control it. Often that particular aura presents itself in my chest, which is my warning sign.

With a simple partial seizure one region of the brain is affected. I do not lose consciousness and I usually remember what happened during the seizure. Simple partial seizures can affect movement, emotions, and our senses. They typically last from a few seconds to a few minutes. They educated me on what was occurring in my situations. Yes, my seizure medication was increased. One bizarre petit-mal seizure occurred as I got into the car to drive a short distance. When I sat down the car smelled grossly of diarrhea. I looked around and didn't see any outward signs. Who drove my car last? Was this person sick? I kept driving. The odor stopped with the windows down. All of a sudden the strong sense of gas arose inside the car. I gasped. What is happening now? By the time I got to my destination, which was only about two miles, the odor dissipated. My seizures have a high likelihood of returning when I forget to take a daily nap, am stressed or overloaded with tasks, experience vertigo or balance issues, need increased sleep, have decreased seizure drug levels, have an infection, and worsening aphasia. It's recommended to write down the type of seizure that occurred and the date. This is vital information for the neurologist to have for the treatment regimen. Unfortunately, I do not remember to do this.

I recall the time I was helping provide food at a concession stand during Ryan's high school basketball game. I was in front at first trying to help give food and receive the money. Math is such a struggle and so was simply providing the variety of food available. Shame erupted within me and I began to feel that awkward sensation in my chest. I began to learn what was up. Todd knew what to do and encouraged me to stand in the back and simply scoop up the popcorn. No, I had no idea how to use the popcorn maker but at least I could do something! Helping the team and visitors was very important to me.

Recently, I learned about incredible people with epilepsy that is hard to believe. A few include Michelangelo, Edgar Allen Poe, Joan of Arc, Aristotle, Beethoven, Bobby Jones, Prince, Alexander the Great, George Gershwin, and Thomas Edison.

CHAPTER 10

Abrupt Alterations in Life

Casualties from severe head injuries change people without warning. Will I ever be myself again? I loved reading the book by Margery Williams, *The Velveteen Rabbit*, when my children were young. Throughout the story, I learned that becoming "real" doesn't happen all at once. It is a process which takes a while to grow within you. You can struggle with any physical or emotional breakage with rough edges, and need much guidance. When you are truly "real," how others view you is not based on your appearance physically, emotionally, mentally or spiritually nor your intelligence. Some don't understand the alterations depicted within you but that doesn't take who you truly are away—a powerful concept which took me many years after the accident to begin to understand. I truly embrace and understand the powerful message depicted by the dynamics of the velveteen rabbit.

My life was challenging, disheartening, and painful as if I were sinking through quick sand. Frequent denial of my losses was my way of coping. Denial clouds aspects of my acquired memory loss and therefore distorts my reality. Those who survive a TBI can face effects lasting a few days to disabilities which may last the rest of their lives. Effects of TBI can include impaired thinking or memory, movement, sensation (e.g., vision or hearing), or emotional functioning (e.g., personality changes, depression). These issues not only affect individuals but can have lasting effects on families and communities.

Whether we like it or not, post-traumatic stress disorder may also worm its way into our existence. The physical dysfunction may include seizures, headaches, fatigue, sensory loss, sexual dysfunction, flashbacks, nightmares, and difficulty sleeping. Diminished cognitive function can include memory loss and issues with problem solving, decision making, judgment, concentration and organization. Behavioral alterations I feel are the most challenging. These include depression, anxiety, stress, aggression, missing social cues, frustration, mood swings, difficulty relating, reduced self-esteem, lack of emotional control, becoming easily startled, and having frightening thoughts.

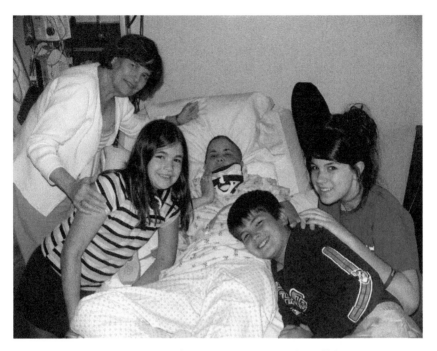

Me, Mom, Meghan 14, Ryan 11, and Molly 8

The family of survivors struggle with incredible loss.
Throughout my hospitalization, my children were just plain
scared and needed the assurance that I was going to be "fine."
After I came home from the hospital, it became apparent that
even the most simple of activities challenged me. I'm not the
mother or wife that I was before the accident since a great
piece of me is gone. My family wants me back, but I'm not the
same person anymore. My children have been so angry and
frustrated. Early on they used harsh, painful words that spun
me into a hurricane. I was described as "You're stupid, dumb,
disgusting, useless, and never helpful." They accused me of
behaving like a teenager! And I was told, "Mom, I'm not as
close to you now as I was before. You make so many mistakes!"
"Since you don't have a job, you're now the family maid." It
was heart wrenching for me to hear these words. Despite the

anguish that all of us were experiencing, our family chose not to participate in family counseling. The rehabilitation hospital never mentioned how essential it was for the family to understand my injury and develop some coping strategies. This was a huge mistake. Everyone could have adjusted more quickly with outside help in understanding the injury and processing our feelings. I believe a part of them felt that counseling would bring on more misery trying to further understand the reality of brain injury. Meghan as an adolescent hated going to see a counselor. She felt no person had the right to barge into her life telling her what to feel and how to act, especially since the counselor would be a stranger. My children's life was so altered, demeaned in a sense, and their pride was lost.

At this point I strongly considered living alone. My parenting ability was transformed significantly, and I felt lost and incapable. I thought perhaps parenting was twice as hard for survivors. When I asked, a professional stated, "Bridgid, it's six to ten times harder to be a parent than previously." Ouch! Another aspect of my life's journey over which I had no control.

The process of healing a family is often a slow pathway to regain wholeness. Weekly to monthly family assessment and treatment is crucial. Children can often feel denial, panic, fear of the future, isolation, and emotional struggles such as shock, anger, guilt, and sadness. This varies throughout their ages. Molly at eight years of age taught me how to remember simple words! Utter sadness overwhelms me when I think about the loss of my ability to assist with my children's homework, play certain games, and cook a meal effectively. Homework was very challenging for me, even when I was trying to help Molly in elementary school! This was embarrassing and demeaning since, prior to this brain injury, I was a good speller and understood the demands of elementary and high school homework and could effectively use a computer. How did this make my children feel? They are much more intelligent than I am now.

Molly is incredibly independent today and I now know why. A short while ago she came out of her bedroom with a tiny tear in one eye. She asked if I wanted to know what just happened. Molly slipped on her bed forcefully and unfortunately her knee popped out! With her amazing endurance she pushed her knee back inward and walked out to show me! Yes, my mouth hung open especially when she smiled at me! My heart was tender when she was recently beautifully riding a galloping horse over an equestrian fence. Molly inspires me. I asked to ride as well and dreamed of me cantering with the horse. She refused and only let me ride when she pulled the horse. She knew that I shouldn't ride without a helmet and my titanium plate. I continued to beg. She acted like she was in charge and stated, "I'm watching over you, Mom." In some ways she was on her own learning and living very quickly at eight years of age. Todd visualized her as a "mother" since I was a child at that time.

My memory loss is so hard on my family. I often forget what they tell me, where and when I'm supposed to be somewhere and who's driving whom? When I play simple games with my children, I forget how to play, I am slower than I was previously, and usually do not win or excel in my understanding or knowledge of the game. Sometimes, Molly would share how slow I was and shocked that I forgot the rules or process of the game. Therefore, she rarely wants to play games with me anymore.

I have a tendency to accidently burn myself when cooking. The children just stare at me looking as if they wonder if I will ever succeed. I forget a recipe that I knew previously in my mind. I need to read a recipe several times, slowly, to comprehend the steps of the cooking process. Sometimes I still make mistakes cooking. Ryan often asks me if I put the right ingredients he likes in the food. Evidently these challenges are common among people who have traumatic brain injury, but I sometimes feel as though I have senile dementia. People often share the normalcy of my experience since it occurs in their own lives. To the contrary, this is not who I was before and I'm not in my eighties.

Noise in and of itself greatly impacts my ability to focus, concentrate, and remember the things I am attempting to complete. Gee, there is no noise in a family of five! My family resented my excessive fatigue and how it impacted my ability to attend all their school or sport's related events. Mood swings often fall into my pathway, ones that I can't control. My sensitivity to things resembles the look and feeling of lightning. Tears so easily come my way. The largest area of my brain trauma was in the temporal lobe. This is our memory and emotional center. The kids hate when I cry if they're telling me a joke and I don't understand the humor. They always watch my face and say, "Here you go. You're going to cry again." Some laugh and ridicule. I often head to my room when I feel ridiculed. They watch my emotional reaction to so many endeavors. I've learned over time how to let go of both of our reactions and try to understand the anger that they still feel.

I lack the ability to assist with our financial issues which I easily understood previously. I no longer understand when payments are due, what we pay for and why, and have trouble with simple adding and subtracting! Recently, I needed to obtain the total cost of a meal for three people, each priced at thirty four dollars. A calculator was not available, so I tried to accomplish the task myself. I added thirty-four plus three instead of multiplying thirty-four times three. The answer made no sense to me. I then thought to view the internet's answer to this problem. I discovered that the value was so much higher than mine. Why? I slowly determined that I should have multiplied. Recalling how to multiply took me awhile but, once I was able to do so, I was shocked to see how the cost was for meals for three people. What truly is my role?

Divorce rates are high when one spouse has sustained a brain injury. Fortunately, the divorce rate is lower for couples married for a long time before the accident. Todd and I had been married for eighteen years at the time of my accident. Todd is such a kind, patient, calm, educated, nurturing man who has stuck by me and helped our family heal from this tragedy. He truly is my advocate! He still believes, honors, and respects me for who I am today! We recently celebrated our 25th wedding anniversary, an indispensable illustration that defines how miracles never cease.

CHAPTER 11

Mental Illness Allergy

Brain injury survivors have a two times higher risk of major depression, suicidal ideation, anxiety disorders, PTSD, obsessive compulsive disorders, and substance abuse. These issues have a tendency to increase two to eight years and more following the initial brain trauma. They can emerge within you like a pit bull! So many assume all emotional issues stop after rehabilitation. Guess what, whether we like it or not, this is a chronic disease! Mayo Clinic defines major depression as a "persistent feeling of sadness and loss of interest and affects how you think, feel and behave and can lead to a variety of emotional and physical problems." Neuropsychologists truly understand the major depression issues involved following traumatic brain injury. I have faced many of the above heart-wrenching challenges. Suicidal ideation could erupt at times when I've spoken and questioned God. "I am warped and failing. I have lost my previous relationship with my family and friends. My wonderful career is lost. Why am I still here? What is my purpose in life now?"

One dreadfully cold winter was one of the times that major depression soared within me. Thoughts of death arose. My career had slipped away and I never felt it would return to my being. Around this time, Husam, a Jordanian father, amazingly called me at home during a time when my spirit was so lost and suffering. I provided care to his three children as they were uninsured and had no primary care provider. Husam and his wife thanked me for the incredible care I gave their family. Husam stated, "We came back to the United States because people like you make the world more beautiful. In my life experience we will never forget you. You are an angel to us and a very strong woman in your survival from traumatic brain injury." I was stunned that they remembered me and cried so long and hard at what he shared with me. In addition, a woman called my name and approached me in a grocery store with a beautiful smile and hugged me. I cared for her disabled child. With tears, she displayed her gratitude for receiving exceptional care for both her child and herself. Messages were sent my way at such challenging times. I just needed to truly listen. Giving up was not necessary to any extent!

Medication and counseling are essential. There are support groups for family and advocates as well as survivors, which I feel are crucial. There is tremendous value in receiving education about brain injury, validation for your feelings and experiences, and vital support from those who truly understand.

It has been eight years since my accident. Today I focus away from my own self-pity but still can ruminate about all the suffering my family has endured. Emotional pain is the most challenging to heal from and can take five to ten years or longer to process. Families of those with brain injury may feel they are living with a very different person, mirroring a stranger. They may become detached from one another, which has been a very sad sight for me to witness. Family roles and responsibilities and feelings about their life change just like seeing my eight-year-old re-teaching games, how to use a microwave, and appropriate words to use. Did she feel like my mother at that time? Did my helplessness force her to be an independent young girl? Such sorrow emerges within my spirit. But disabilities don't take away all our abilities to heal, and to adapt and move forward. I just have to remember that every day I get a little bit better.

Brain injury conferences provide remarkable opportunities to learn. So much of what I've been educated about has been learned at conferences. I cried often as professionals, survivors, and family members shared such valuable information about their experiences-things that I frequently experienced myself- especially emotions. How powerful it is when I realized, no, I hadn't lost my mind. My mom has always gone with me and would recall so much of the information that I frequently forgot. Mom would often read personal survivor stories to me, which was so ministering. My sister Rachel gave me a CD of the book *Over My Head* written by Claudia Osborn. Hearing a book written by a physician who sustained a brain injury from a bike accident was very powerful because of the similarities in both our stories. Wow!

CHAPTER 12

Vacuuming the Grass

Some of the most challenging aspects I continue to struggle with are aphasia and memory loss. When I began speaking following my accident, I could only verbalize a few words at a time and often some of the words were not accurate. Many who were not familiar with aphasia or brain injury would give me a confused look and some would laugh when they heard me speak. Ugh. Such sadness, hurt and loss emerged within me. In the midst of completing two years of speech therapy three times a week, my aphasia greatly improved.

Today, aphasia affects me in the following ways. I continue having difficulty speaking effectively and recognizing the name of basic objects, streets, animals, food, you name it. I often ask Ryan to "mow the lawn" during a snowstorm when I intended to say "shovel the snow;" or "vacuum the grass" when I intended to say "mow."

One of the essentials in working with someone like me who has aphasia is to give me a chance to try the word myself. It is demeaning to directly give me the word right away. Initially, I may try to describe the word to tell you things which remind me of or resemble the word. If I am still challenged, I will then ask for the first letter of the word and thus will keep on trying. If my aphasia persists, it is sufficient to tell me the word at this time. Often we can somehow describe the word in certain ways, such as "scrub" when we really want to say "laundry."

When I'm stressed about something, such as meeting people for the first time, my aphasia is worse than usual. I often tap my throat when I can't get the words, as if they will understand my disabilities, which is so frequently untrue. Today I tried to say "railroad track" but the word that came through slowly was "tide." To this day, I still struggle with remembering words and often sound as if I made up the words.

Many months after my discharge, I overheard my niece say to Meghan, "Your mom talks like a baby." These words were intense and dreadful for me to hear. I wish I could have heard my daughter's response or seen the look on her face. Then again, she probably nodded yes and felt the same way.

I can only tolerate reading one or two pages of easy literature at a time, and do best when it is written in a simple way, such as a sixth-grade level. I am told by my therapists that I progressed from third grade to ninth grade level in my reading ability when I was taking speech therapy. I read slowly and many times lose my memory of what I just read. Speech therapists encouraged me to read a few pages two to three times and highlight the important messages of particular sentences.

The first time I tried to use a computer I was at St. Luke's Hospital during inpatient rehabilitation. Todd wanted me to see all the many emails I received since my accident.

He was shocked that I remembered the password. I was shocked by the incredible number of emails I had received from wonderful colleagues and friends. I could not read for very long since this life was so very new to me. I felt frightened and lost. Today, when I am using the computer to write, say this book, I misspell so many words. I will look at a word I wrote and wonder what the heck this is! Sentences are not accurate. Even when I have spelled a word correctly, I continue to doubt myself. I often forget how to type what I'm feeling. Frustration and anger erupt in my spirit. But if I give myself a "time out," I can return to my project refreshed and read and understand whatever was challenging me! The power of a time out (traditionally reserved for toddlers) is so necessary for me even though I'm an adult. I so appreciate this tip I learned from speech therapists.

Recently, I was looking for an easy way to make a shrimp recipe on the Internet and I typed "shrimp resume." Today, when I am lost in my comprehension, I often ask Todd or my children how to spell a particular word. For instance, I will misspell the word "apply." It takes me awhile but I try to write apply by spelling "aploe." Why does my brain proceed as it does? The other day, I was asked how to spell Christmas. I lost my memory despite successfully writing the first three letters, "Chr." "Inissully," no I mean "enitaly." It is not until after I type, those letters don't appear correct. The computer's spell check of the word is often confused in interpreting what I am trying to spell. Out of my frustration, I need a time out. "Eatting breckfast" is what I need as this "descrepincy" continues. I've worked on this paragraph for an hour, a headache occurs and my brain won't allow me to proceed any further. Now I let it go and accept reality. I have improved and will not stop trying.

Fortunately, I have developed a sense of humor about the words I repeatedly say incorrectly-like "vacuuming the grass." Thank God I can finally laugh despite so many of my cognitive challenges! Todd generally knows what I'm talking about.

And speaking of grass...I love to cut the grass, but Todd prefers that I don't cut the grass, as our lawn is seven-tenths of an acre which includes areas with small hills which challenge my sense of balance. Whether I like it or not or remember, I continue to have balance issues when I'm walking or going up or down stairs. I love to wear tennis shoes when I'm mowing the lawn. Todd is concerned and feels that tennis shoes aren't supportive enough for me in walking and pushing a mower. My misjudgment of the safety issues don't occur until I mow on wet grass wearing tennis shoes.

There is a degree of power involved in starting a challenging lawn mower as it pushes me through anger and then steadily moves me forward cutting the long grass that needs "cleaning and polishing." In a way, this symbolizes many of my life's learning and healing lessons. I have always loved being outside working within nature, taking care of our flowers and the yard, for as long as I can remember. I have even wanted to attempt "showering" a small tree that had died. Oops! The words I should have used, "Chainsawing a tree," which Todd thought was ludicrous and wouldn't allow it.

The other day, Todd was surprised that I could get the lawnmowers to start. They are challenging to start and don't work well. My smiles begin as I love feeling free and in control of something that I could care for such as the grass. I wore my usual tennis shoes despite Todd's insistence that I wear cleats. I didn't have cleats. My feet are the smallest in our family so I couldn't wear Ryan's size 13 cleats. I assumed that since the sun had shined for a few days, the grass was dry. I have no memory that morning grass could be wet. As

I approached a small hill, I began walking and pushing the mower in a downward pattern from side to side. The front wheel drive of the mower wasn't working but I was able to push it forward with my strength. This is another attribute of mine that surprises Todd. At one point the grass appeared mildly moist, but I did not pay any attention or respond, as I guess I should have. Unfortunately, I slid and fell to my side. I was worried I'd get sliced from the blade. Once on the ground, I remembered to let go of the mower. Todd told me a day or two earlier to do this if I ever fell. In the midst of falling, I let it go, assuming it would continue all the way down the trail. Thank God I witnessed it gradually stop and shut off.

I was amazed and shocked this occurred, but once again I was given another warning message which I paid no attention to or didn't remember. Yes, I can be a pistol at times, thinking I can be in charge of doing so many things. Yes, another life learning lesson I'm discovering, accepting and attempting to alter and appreciate. Todd said I could no longer mow without wearing cleats. He insisted we purchase cleats that very same day. Again I made excuses and said that we didn't need to go that day. I also didn't want to spend that kind of money. Regardless, we headed to a sporting goods store. Todd told me to have them measure my shoe size in the children's section! Smiles and laughter came over me, as I found this process hilarious. My daughter Molly was with us and looked at me strangely. I measured a size 4 in the children's shoe sizes. The man who was helping me smiled a great deal as he had never seen an adult woman trying on kid's shoes! I imagine the further shock in his head as he was working with a woman of my age trying on cleats! When size 4 cleats fit, he smiled and said, "You can now play soccer!" With laughter, I mentioned that I could now kick a football even better. Ryan, a football player, witnessed me kick a football far and high and his eyes widened and mouth hung open out of utter shock. Was this his mom?

The next day, I finished mowing the grass with my cleats on. Those shoes were amazing and provided security in running and kicking football and soccer ball! I felt such strength and control in holding onto the ground beneath me. I smiled when I finished the lawn and then laughed when I noticed that I had sweat on my face, something I've never experienced before. I respect Todd's insistence that I wear my cleats, but I will still need continual reminders. I have a hard time waiting for spring to return to mow and kick a football again!

CHAPTER 13

Where Did My Memory Go?

In addition to the challenges of aphasia, I must also contend with memory loss. Memory loss is very common among brain injury survivors; and it makes me feel better to know that I am not alone in my challenges. Reading about and meeting other survivors provides tremendous validation of the challenges I face. I remain challenged to completely understand and remember what people say to me. The slower a person speaks to me significantly enhances my ability to understand their intention of the conversation. A decreased tone of the voice and minimizing knowledge of the subject guide me as well. I always forget the names of people and how I met them. In order for me to remember their names, I need to practice saying their names numerous times before it is somewhat obtained in my brain. Generally, I need to see people several times to understand where, how, and why I met them. Sometimes I recognize the sound of their voice, which potentially links me to my previous interaction with them. My brain mutates itself all over the place in so many different directions at one time.

I frequently lose and forget where objects, such as a cell phone, were placed. Therefore, people have a challenging time reaching me. No, for me this was not my behavior before the accident and is currently not a symptom of pre-senile dementia or menopause! I have lost so many items and recently discovered they are sometimes located in the garbage can—especially the cat litter scooper! Perhaps my brain thinks the cat litter scoopers themselves are garbage. Yes, we've had to purchase several cat litter scoopers. Can you guess where I found the last one? I continue to check the garbage can for any lost item when it is not too odorous or disgusting! The kids will always ask me, "Mom, did you throw my red shirt away?" I reply, "Of course not!" "Mom, are you sure?" Sometimes when I go outside, I stand there silently alone on the lawn waiting and wondering why I'm there. My mind continues to display such confusion when either I'm in the house, grocery store, driving or helping out at my children's school function.

One of my most embarrassing moments occurred when I was doing laundry. I went to pull out the clothing from the washer. When I opened the door, a flattened, scattered Playtex container and tampons showed themselves. All the tampons were still covered with a plastic wrapper so naturally I tried to save them for reuse, especially considering the cost! When I reached the bottom of the washed clothes I discovered a full plastic bag of brownie mix. What on earth? I was confused and flustered and in utter shock. The laundry that I was washing was mainly Ryan's. This was a big deal since he finally gave me clothing items to wash at the end of junior high school. Yes, they were stranded in his locker all year. Yikes!

Around the time that I was doing the laundry, Ryan was taking a German class and was required to make an authentic German dessert. Since I had forgotten how and what he made, I asked Ryan what he needed for the recipe. Perhaps Ryan had left the brownie mix in the clothing from his locker? This made no sense at all. I asked Ryan what all had occurred. Ryan looked at me in a confused stare, shocked that I couldn't remember and said, "Mom, we made the dessert at home and did not use brownie mix." "No, I have not taken any brownie mix to school!" I have a tendency to forget putting washed clothes into the dryer or place items in the dryer that I was asked numerous times not to mechanically dry! What on earth occurred that I stuffed brownie mix in the washer? That mix stayed in the plastic container bag but I wasn't sure if I should still use it.

The worst episode occurred when I began to collect clothing from the washer to directly place in the dryer. When I got near the bottom of the load I noticed a flat small brown and black rectangular shaped item. I had forgotten to put on my glasses, therefore, I was clueless with untreated vision. I went to place it in the dryer but as I lifted it closer to my eyes, I screeched and nearly vomited as I witnessed a smashed dead mouse! How on earth did that mouse get into my washer? Yes, we have mice in our home at times but never in the washer! I worried about mice enjoying Molly's bedroom but I wasn't washing her clothes. Why did the mouse arrive in my own laundry basket? What attracted it? Or did it somehow climb in the washer? Molly denies that she put the mouse in the laundry basket. I could picture her loving to do that. Did I somehow in some strange way place the mouse, tampons, brownie mix in my washer? At this point, I felt as if I had truly lost my mind. As time has moved on, I can now truly laugh at these hysterical brain farts.

Occasionally, I forget to take my seizure medication and vitamins, which I keep in the kitchen where I am more likely to see them, especially since they are prescribed twice a day. I do not realize I missed taking my medication until later in the afternoon, early evening, or the next day. I use a daily labeled medication dispensing container, but I often forget what day of the week it actually is. In addition, I cannot remember what is supposed to happen today even though I was told yesterday and it was written the night before on two different calendars. This is a good example of one of the types of situations that make my children so upset. Then, I become angry and sad at myself.

My memory loss and continued balance issues present themselves when I do not notice or recall a curb or steps going downward. On one occasion, as I walked away from the middle of a podium, I thought that I was walking down a few steps, which were not there. Unfortunately, the length to the ground was two to three feet from the floor. I swooped downward and a woman who was close by tried to grab me but I somehow balanced myself! Perhaps this was another angelic response to prevent me from the falling. I've fallen as I hiked on wooden trails. I lose my balance and can't seem to identify the walking area below me. I've walked on a sidewalk where the curb was altered for the handicapped and fallen into the street. I often slip up and especially down walking on sports bleachers. I need to continue to remember to always hold on to the handle bar when I walk up or down steps. I'm so grateful that I haven't broken any bones. Frequently I'm asked, "How did you get your bruises?" Bleeding and bruising can occur after such a simple bump. If I'm with Todd, he always reminds me how to walk effectively and ideally with someone near me. He always holds my hands.

Being able to drive a car on my own again during those times when I am seizure free for six months brings me such joy, freedom, and independence. Unfortunately, I often forget where I parked the car or put the car keys. To help me remember where I've parked, I stare at a letter of the store's name and park in that region. I challenge my brain to try to recall where I was parked. On occasion, I still have to engage the car's device that activates the horn to guide me in the right direction. My worst episode occurred as I drove the car into the garage, parked, shut the garage door, and headed into the house. There was a strange noise and I didn't know where it came from. I stepped into the garage and I gasped as the car was still running! I was frightened to even share this with Todd.

When I drive on a two-way street and a large truck passes by me, my heart rate begins to rise. When a biker is biking on the road next to me, I need to deep breathe and tell myself, this fear shall pass.

One time, I drove the incorrect way on a one-way street. I was alerted of my error by a person driving towards me. I was not intoxicated but terrified of being pulled over. This triggers anxiety. I try to deep breathe slowly. "Remember, Bridgid, you have angels right here with you." I have to always remember that I have an angel hanging from the mirror in my car, which states *faith brings miracles*. Before I drive my car, I ask those precious angels for protection, guidance and safety. Molly often doesn't like me driving when she's a passenger. She always sternly talks to me about my driving skills that aren't perfect. She acts as if she's the mother of a teenager. Perhaps her anxiety and anger erupt when I'm in charge of things I couldn't do earlier in my recovery. Family members can have a hard time letting go of what frightened them before.

My family says that I look so much better without glasses and prefer me to remove them for pictures. I forgot that I've tried to put on contacts previously. The optometrist shared, "Bridgid, you've tried this before and you didn't want to continue wearing them due to your hand tremors in applying them and memory loss of the procedures." I replied, "Oh. Can I try again?" Hilarious episodes have occurred with my continuous attempts to utilize contact lenses effectively. Unfortunately, I often forget exactly what I was instructed to do. Once I found a contact in a bowl of the grapefruit I had eaten. Didn't notice it was in there until I started to drink the grapefruit juice! I have gone into the optometrist's office several times with tears of sadness and frustration. Why couldn't I go back to how I looked before the accident? I didn't want to quit trying. Who cares that it took me nine months to effectively use contacts. The optometrist's staff shared that they had never seen a patient take nine months to understand and complete the process! I'm not quitting, even when I still make mistakes. It really helps me when I pray before I insert or remove the contacts! Awesome!

CHAPTER 14

Angels Among Us

For as long as I can remember, I have always believed in the presence of angels among us protecting, supporting, educating, loving, and never leaving our side. God sends them our way with powerful messages and miracles to our soul. And while I have suffered periods of sadness, discouragement and self-pity since my accident, I know that angels sent many adults, children, and animals my way to assist in my healing and enlightening me with my life's purpose. I would like to share some of my experiences with you.

So many incredible angelic encounters have ventured into my life. When I was pregnant with my second child, Ryan, Meghan, nearly three years old at the time, described that angels were talking to her. Angels told Meghan that Ryan was a boy and that he was going to be born early. Ryan was born three weeks early. He shocked the obstetrician that he truly was nine pounds, as my physical body did not reveal him at this size. I was blown away with Meghan's beautiful angelic experience.

One snowing, blustery December day, Todd and I and our two small children ventured to Dubuque, Iowa, to celebrate the holidays with family and friends. On the way, we stopped at a restaurant in Cedar Rapids to meet up with college friends and their families. The snow was coming down heavily but we neglected to notice since we were absorbed in reminiscing about old times. Time passed quickly and the snow accumulated rapidly. Although there were several inches of snow on the ground when we left Cedar Rapids, I felt confident in Todd's driving ability and the durability of our minivan traveling in all kinds of weather.

The highway was crowded with folks traveling to see their loved ones. We could only safely travel about 40 mph on the highway. The wind and snow created slippery driving conditions and the visibility was less than a mile. I was grateful to see that my children, Meghan (three) and Ryan (one), had fallen fast asleep in their car seats. Meghan was very challenging to take on road trips. She hated to be strapped in a car seat. Therefore, I was grateful she was asleep.

I was enjoying the peace and quiet when all of a sudden I heard a loud voice inside my ears saying, "Check the car seats!" Without thinking much about it, I instinctively followed the directions, unfastened my seatbelt, and went back to check the children's car seats. Meghan's car seat was securely fastened but to my surprise, Ryan's seatbelt was not fastened to the car seat! I was shocked as to why the seatbelt had become unfastened. I quickly refastened it and returned to my own seat and buckled in. The beat of my heart was pounding quickly. No sooner had I buckled myself in my chair than Todd spun quickly across the highway and merged onto a shoulder above a ditch. He tried desperately to maneuver the van in a quick motion to get the van back and away from the ditch, spinning 360 degrees across the highway! The van came to a halt only a foot away from the ditch! I turned to check on the children and found them still sound asleep! My adrenaline soared. I recalled seeing many cars only moments earlier in the oncoming lane that we just spun through! Where were other cars now? Who told me to check the children's car seats? The experience instantly made me cry and I began reciting the Lord's Prayer in gratitude for the blessings our angels bestow on us.

When Ryan was two and a half years old and Meghan was five, she approached me with a tender nature. Angels told her that I was going to have another baby girl. The muscles around my eyes and forehead erupted upward. I had never planned to have another child and thus was stunned. I didn't reflect on using the process needed to promote this! Therefore, I chuckled with Meghan's startling news. Smiles emerged regarding her poor understanding of the reality of such an illusion. Two weeks later I neglected to maintain my consistent menstrual period. When I decided to double check the unlikelihood of pregnancy, my mouth and eyes opened largely in a bit of a panic, as the pregnancy test was positive! How on earth could this have happened? Another miracle was sent my way.

We successfully raised three children while I was working as a pediatric nurse practitioner providing primary care to uninsured students in the Cedar Rapids School District. I embraced my pregnancy and then another challenge emerged. In early June 1999, my family was in Minneapolis, Minnesota, for my sister Kathleen's wedding. As a bridesmaid, I unfortunately discovered that my dress size was prepared too tight and poorly adjusted. Thank God we found a wonderful woman who re-formed dresses that I thought were impossible to alter. She was shocked how poorly my dress was initially prepared. Once the dress was taken care of, we practiced our roles at the church.

Unexpectedly, my abdomen and uterus started to swirl while we were rehearsing. I was shocked and denied the reality of truly having contractions. I was only six months pregnant! Todd brushed it off as well, which wasn't helpful. Suddenly I realized that I needed to get to the hospital ASAP, as I was in preterm labor! I spent the night alone in the hospital worrying with fear. I'm grateful I was discharged with the expectation that I was now on bed rest! I needed a wheelchair. Thank God that the obstetrician allowed me to walk up and down the aisle during Kathleen and Paul's wedding! I recall my dad attempting to walk me down the steps to get to his car when I was discharged. The obstetric nurse was upset and gave him a wheelchair stressing that I was on bed rest until Molly's birth. Piece of cake with already having two children. Molly was born one month early but completely healthy and weighing seven pounds and one ounce.

Ryan had a tendency to get injured during high school football practice. One practice he was running very quickly and went through an unnoticed dip in the ground. He was thrown and landed on his right knee. Shortly after this occurred, I was called by a physical therapist who asked me to come as soon as I could to West High School. I was afraid and thus prayed on my way. When I arrived I could see indications on Ryan's face that he was in pain. An ice bag was on his elevated right knee. She didn't look at me directly but stated that she thought he had torn his anterior cruciate ligament (ACL), a ligament in the knee that crosses from the underside of the femur (the thigh bone) to the top of the tibia (the bigger bone in the lower leg) (www.medicinenet. com). Unfortunately, surgery is necessary with ACL injury. I looked at her and prayed to the angels saying, "I believe that the injury would be less than this." She stated, "Well, it could be a meniscus injury," which reduces the severity. Ryan saw a sports medicine physician who stated that Ryan tore his ACL but would validate it by a MRI. I saw the tears begin in Ryan's eyes. I continued to pray and asked both grandparents if they would as well. Our cat Angel climbed up on my bed where Ryan was laying and began to lick his right knee for healing. You know, I can't remember why I named her Angel.

When I contacted the physician the next day he, stated, "I can't believe this! I'm shocked as Ryan only suffered a right tibial plateau fracture." Therefore, he didn't need surgery and was unable to walk for only six weeks. With the ACL surgery he would have been unable to walk for nine months! After I talked to the physician, I gave Ryan the phone because of my aphasia. I loved seeing the smile on his face. When he hung up the phone I started jumping up and down squealing in our screened in porch. Ryan gave me a smile and then a disturbed look saying, "Mom, don't do that. What will the neighbors think?" Quite frankly at this point in my life I really don't care. Way to go, angels!

CHAPTER 15

Today's Miracle

Prior to my final brain surgery to place a titanium plate in my blank skull, I began having altered vision changes. Dr. Ryken recommended I see a neuro-ophthalmologist. These are physicians who are both neurologist and ophthalmologist specializing in diseases affecting vision that originate from the nervous system, such as brain trauma. The parietal lobe and occipital lobe (visual center of the brain) of my brain were also impacted, as they merge in an alignment with the temporal and frontal lobe regions.

As I dove into the numerous vision evaluations, my aunt Katie was present with me. I passed the intensive visual field testing and had excellent vision, 20/20 in both eyes. My eyeballs were fine and there was no permanent damage for visual impairment. When I completed the lengthy testing, I went to see Dr. Lee, a neuro-ophthalmologist. Silently, Dr. Lee, looked at me and then my CT scans. As he returned to look directly at me, his eyes were wide and shocking words erupted from his mouth. He slightly shook his head and said, "Bridgid, I can hardly believe we are standing here talking to each other! You are a miracle!" Katie's mouth hung open while she looked at me in such astonishment saying, "See, Bridgid, I told you! You are a miracle!"

I looked back at Katie with my bright green eyes spread open. My upper body shuttered backward as if I was in shock. Really? What on earth do you mean? I needed an abundant answer to this word, "miracle." Dr. Lee was the first and only physician who ever said this. Many others did but not a physician! In lieu of my incredible status he recommended that I could proceed with the titanium mesh replacement surgery. I did not need any further vision testing unless this changes.

Months following the placement of my titanium plate, I motioned through life in a very slow process. Despite all the blessings and encouragement I received, I still struggled emotionally as I continued to realize that I was not returning back to the woman I was before. Did TBI really venture into my life to cause such disruptions to our family? Why? Explain this to me, God, as I don't understand. Was I at fault in some way that caused the bicycle accident? I needlessly questioned and misunderstand the word, 'miracle' and wondered if God was truly involved. I felt lost.

Prior to my accident, I was encouraged by my dear friend Jane to visit with a woman named Paulette Lucas, a clairvoyant spiritual counselor. Paulette has provided clairvoyant readings for over twenty years and works through spirit guides, angels, and those who passed over. Being counseled by someone skilled with spiritual clairvoyance was a whole new realm of adventure in my life. Once I worked through my fear, I acquired the courage to receive a reading from Paulette. I was astounded and mesmerized with the validity of all that Paulette shared with me. My sister-in-law, Lori, and I attended a class which nurtured and guided those grieving from the loss of a loved one. Lori and my experiences were profound as it was eye-opening and incredibly healing.

While many people dispute the validity of clairvoyance, I was desperate for answers…anything that could put my mind at rest. I went forward and contacted Paulette. During our conversation, Paulette shared that during my initial hospitalization three angels were around my head telling me so gently and lovingly that I was dying. There was no fear within me. The angels were Archangel Raphael, Archangel Haniel, and Archangel Metatron. They expressed that they will continuously be by my side and that I will never be alone. I will be in peace. Archangels watch over and heal and are designed as administrators to the guardian angels. Archangel Raphael is a chief healing angel for all of creation. His name means "God heals." Raphael is also an educator to health care professionals. Raphael is supported through Christianity, Judaism, and Islam. Archangel Haniel is an angel of God's grace. Haniel helps us return to our genuine state of existence. Her God-given energy guides us to reorient ourselves to our true and natural state of grace and thus return to our purity of our God-given soul. Archangel Metatron is the Angel of the Light. He focuses on our life's priority, organization and motivation. Presently in utter amazement, I was stunned to learn that Metratron is an angel colleague who gives support for writers!

Apparently, as I listened to the angels' intentions, I waited for a moment before I responded. I stated, "Can we talk about this?" They tuned in willingly to hear me express, "I love my husband and children so very much and I enjoy helping other's heal. Is there any way I could stay longer in this realm of being?" The archangels pondered in their decision as they were communicating with the Divine. In time they verbalized,

"Bridgid, you may remain in your physical body and return. Know that it will take a great deal of time and support to help you heal in your journey." I choose to believe in the validity of all that Paulette shared with me. It has helped me understand that my life was spared because God has a purpose for my life. To this day, I continue to feel utterly astonished by the celestial intervention of my trauma. I can't begin to say how very grateful I am to God, the angelic messengers and health care providers delivering such tremendous healing.

CHAPTER 16

Angelic Messages from Animal Spirit Guides

I have always loved birds and initially learned how to attract them with bird seed on my small apartment deck which I could easily visualize through a large window. My dad mentioned to me that I would never encounter a bird based on where the deck was located as a fourth of the deck was covered with the apartment wall. Therefore, a bird could only see half of the deck. I didn't let that stop me. One bright morning in May 1990, a beautiful dove amazingly appeared on my small deck. My mouth hung open in shock, especially since I had not put bird seed on the deck yet! I had never seen a dove before. The dove was light grey and slightly brown with a beige chest and black spots on its wings. The wings themselves can make an unusual whistling sound upon take-off and landing.

Doves have an amazing ability to soar up to 55 mph. This dove arose up and down near me several times and then walked back and forth looking at me through my window. Tears emerged with shock but also sadness. While the dove was present on my deck, I received a heart-wrenching phone call. My paternal grandmother Bede, one whom I adored, died earlier that morning. My dear grandma had been suffering from lung cancer one year following the death of her husband, Grandpa Virgil. I was told that this type of dove was called a "morning dove'," which is how I expected it to be spelled, as if it was a morning riser. Many years later, I was shocked when my father-in-law, Dick, shared with me that it is spelled "mourning" dove. I saw this dove on my deck as a divine messenger sent to acknowledge Grandma's death. When I researched information regarding the dove, I found a book, *Animal Sprit Guide,* by Steven Farmer, PhD which is very intriguing. Steven wrote that, if a dove shows itself around you, several messages are being sent your way. The message that moved me stated, "The soul of someone who's recently passed is making a smooth, peaceful and joyous transition." How very profound.

On July 4, 2000, my thirty-six-year-old brother-in-law, Bill, died following a challenging battle with a glioblastoma brain tumor. I highly recommended that Bill receive his brain surgery at the University of Iowa Hospitals and Clinics (UIHC). They chose UIHC and interestingly enough, Bill had the same wonderful neurosurgeon that I did, Dr. Tim Ryken. Bill lived longer than the six months the physicians predicted. He was a hardworking, generous, and kind-hearted man who is missed dearly. He left behind his wife Lori, to whom he was married thirteen years, and three precious daughters: Jenny, Katie, and Kimberly. Lori and I have always had a dear connection and special bond. We have embraced and loved a connection with angels for such a long time. At that time, Jenny was twelve years old, Kaitlyn ten, and Kimberly six. Children are often the forgotten mourners after the death of a family member. I have always felt a special connection with my nieces. I prayed for a way that they could somehow be a part of Bill's wake. Children provide us with such powerful insight and guidance from the Divine. With inspiration, Jenny, Katie and my eight-year-old daughter Meghan sang the beautiful song "I Will Remember You" by Sarah McLachlan at the wake. Jenny recently shared with me a fuzzy memory she has of Bill's wake. She remembered the name of the song but not what part of this beautiful melody these precious girls sang. I recall the first three paragraphs that they sang, which is written below. This song has incredible verses which honor children's grief experience as well as touch and nurture all who hear them.

I Will Remember You

Sarah McLachlan

I will remember you
Will you remember me?
Don't let your life pass you by
Weep not for the memories

Remember the good times that we had?
I let them slip away from us when things got bad
How clearly I first saw you smilin' in the sun
Wanna feel your warmth upon me, I wanna be the one

I will remember you
Will you remember me?
Don't, let your life pass you by
Weep not for the memories

I'm, so tired but I can't sleep
Standin' on the edge of something much too deep
It's funny how we feel so much but we cannot say a word
We are screaming inside, but we can't be heard

But I will remember you
Will you remember me?
Don't, let your life pass you by
Weep not for the memories

I'm so afraid to love you, but more afraid to lose
Clinging to a past that doesn't let me choose
Once there was a darkness, deep and endless night
You gave me everything you had, oh you gave me light

And I will remember you
Will you remember me?
Don't let your life pass you by
Weep not for the memories

And I will remember you
Will you remember me?
Don't let your life pass you by
Weep not for the memories
Weep not for the memories

The grief that accompanies a major loss can often feel so overwhelming and you feel so hopeless. Yet, even the subtle signs from the spirit world can provide us with great comfort if we open ourselves to trust such a gift. Since Bill's death, I've often encouraged my nieces to observe signs and messages their dad will continue to present to them. Lori feels grateful for the nourishing love and care I provided their family during such a horrendous life experience. I encouraged the children to attend a bereavement support group that ministers to the needs of children. Their sorrow is often overlooked because of the adult's own loss and emotional needs. In my mind, it was not me personally identifying their needs and treatment options but God sending me messages to guide their healing from grief. I shared with my nieces that Bill's presence and a divine message could present themselves in mystical ways such as vision of a particular bird or animal, words other people say, dreams, pictures, music, sounds, and any other entities that remind them of their dad.

On October 5, 2002, my nieces, Jennifer and Kaitlyn, and I ventured forth on an annual camping trip along a beautiful trail at Backbone State Park located in Strawberry Point, Iowa. This was our third year camping together at Backbone and two years since their dad, Bill's death from brain cancer in 2000. I recall saying to others, "I'm sure up for a spiritual experience this weekend!" For two years the girls and I have taken healing nature hikes that leave us invigorated and peaceful. The walk allowed the girls to get in touch with the spirituality that is alive in nature as well as to provide an opportunity to express their feelings associated with the enormous grief they suffered.

We hiked the wooded trails on a crisp autumn day with beautiful leaves flowing on the trees expecting good things to come our way. The sun was shining and the fall foliage portrayed brilliant colors of orange, red, and yellow. We reminisced about such fond memories of our experiences with Bill. Venturing back to the cabin we discovered a beautiful high level of the trail that overlooked the lake below. The scene was picturesque as the beautiful leaves left their imprints on the water's surface. Kaitlyn asked if we could stop, rest, and enjoy the scenery before returning to the cabin. We agreed and sat together allowing our healing tears of grief emerge and fall unrestrained. I put my arms around them and said, "My prayer for you is that your dad will send you signs that he's always present with you."

Very soon after I said this, out of nowhere a unique yet strange-looking butterfly appeared. When its wings were folded together it had the appearance of a dried-up tree leaf but as it unfolded its inner beauty was revealed. The inside of the wings were a bright orange with black flecks on the border and the body was a brilliant green. This was not a monarch. We were stunned as we watched the butterfly make its way toward us. I was shocked and elated when the butterfly landed on my arm! The experience took my breath away and brought immediate tears to my eyes. Never before have I witnessed a butterfly land on a person and stay there!

I was afraid to move my arm for fear of frightening the butterfly. It stayed on my arm for what seemed like a very long time before suddenly flying onto Jennifer's leg. Jennifer was seated next to me. Jennifer gasped and watched intently in amazement as the beautiful butterfly spent at least five minutes with her before it positioned itself on both her and Kaitlyn. The butterfly had two of its legs on Jennifer and the remaining two on Kaitlyn, as if it were intentionally encouraging them to stay connected to one another! Finally, the butterfly flew onto Kaitlyn directly, spending at least another five minutes there. While the butterfly placed itself on each one of us, it looked at us directly and then gently tapped its proboscis on. The proboscis is located between the eyes and used for feeding and sucking nectar. We were being nurtured.

In my mind's eye, a divine message was delivered to take away our pain and place nurturance to our souls, especially to my nieces. In the present day, Jenny feels that both talking to me at Backbone State Park and our miraculous butterfly experience validated her continued grief. The butterfly provided comfort to her in feeling her dad was always present with her and listening to her struggles and needs. In the book *Animal Spirit Guides*, the butterfly symbolizes that your lifestyle is going to change. "In spite of the challenges, you'll get through this transition and as always, know that 'this too shall pass'." Interestingly enough, the same type of butterfly ventured its way to my niece Kimberly and sister-in-law Lori while they were walking on a separate trail across the lake from us. How very powerful!

One fall, we were visiting a farm and noticed kittens for sale. Molly begged for a calico kitten. I was very uncertain but eventually agreed. For whatever reason, I named her Angel. Today though, I now understand that the name "Angel" makes perfect sense. A cat's presence in your life can indicate healing from your inside out. When I first arrived home, I didn't like the fact that I still had the feeding tube in my abdomen. St. Luke's didn't want to remove it since the University of Iowa Hospital put it in. I wanted it out! As I lay on my right side onto my bed at home our cat, a female calico, lays down beside me. She usually follows me everywhere in the home. When she senses that something physically is wrong with one of our family members, she smells the correct area and licks it. As she climbed on the bed she began smelling and scattering her face throughout my abdomen. In a very short time frame, she grabbed the feeding tube in her mouth and tried pulling it out on her own! Although I was nervous, I laughed hysterically. Angel like many animals can be very intuitive and healing. She knew I wanted the removal of this feeding tube!

I loved taking a bus to venture through downtown Kingston, Ontario, Canada. At one point when I was walking I realized that I lost the sweater I was wearing. Dusk began and the temperature was getting cooler and thus I needed that sweater. I began talking to angels asking for their help in me finding that sweater. As I walked toward Lake Ontario River, the Kingston Harbor area looked as if I was there earlier that day. As I approached the harbor I noticed a large, radiant white seagull sitting on the dock. A dark object was lying on the ground in front of the sea gull. The closer I came the seagull began looking at me in such a kind way. Once I was much closer I gasped and then smiled as she was protecting my black sweater that was in front of her. Once I was a few feet from the sea gull she looked at me and flew away. Those blessed angels also helped me find the exact bus I needed to return to the hotel. So many spiritual entities have placed themselves throughout my life. She was showing me that although my sweater was lost, when I speak to the Divine for guidance, lo and behold, my messages are heard and delivered, even by the spirit guides within animals.

Many years before my accident, I was working in a pediatric intensive care unit. I was caring for a young boy who had just undergone a significant heart surgery. In confidence, he shared with me his divine out of body experience, which presented itself during his heart surgery. While in surgery, he felt himself leave his body without fear or remorse and watched the surgeon attending to his heart.

Following this, he flew to where his mother and brother were sitting in the waiting room. He described the exact words they both used and the feelings of fear that they experienced. In addition, he knew what they were wearing and the area of the waiting room in which they were sitting. His mind questioned this experience when talking to me. Was he leaving his body and going to heaven? Miraculously, he returned to his body and successfully completed and recovered from his cardiac surgery. His family was in utter shock as they listened to him amazingly share all of what he heard and visualized during his complete sedation.

Although some don't agree with the aspects of an out-of-body experience (OBE), I sure do. I experienced OBE during the time that I was unconscious and seizing. It was as if it showed me the physiological impact of the grand-mal seizure, a loving woman's voice and tenderness to me and the auras that showed me the symptoms of the intro-duction of a seizure. Often, scientists' impression of OBE is a hallucination caused by various neurological and psy-chological circumstances. Perhaps evidence will be scien-tifically achieved on the basis of the normalcy of OBE and thus the magnificent abundance will be embraced by all.

My belief in OBE occurred once I witnessed the young boy honestly open up to me about his breath-taking epi-sode which occurred during his cardiac surgery. I was so honored he trusted me and it appeared as if he intuitively knew of my belief in his beautiful experience. In my mind, he was not hallucinating, nor was I during my seizure.

CHAPTER 17

The Dynamics of Shamrocks

Shamrocks are the national emblem of Ireland. St. Brigid, a patron saint of Kildare, Ireland, felt that the most beautiful pieces of the land in Ireland were those filled with shamrocks. During the post-war scarcity of food, shamrocks were frequently eaten as a last resort by those malnourished (www.wikipedia.com). Clovers are a valuable survival food as they are high in protein, and are widespread and abundant. The shamrock was traditionally used as a healing resource. St. Brigid is known for her extraordinary spirituality and admin-

istered many healing miracles and fed the poor. Her divine virtues displayed her as a loving, kind, and compassionate woman, especially to those impoverished. She embraces and acknowledges the crucial need the body and spirit desire to be interlaced. St. Brigid helps to increase our fearlessness and gives guidance to discover our life's purpose. St. Brigid's Feast Day is celebrated on February 1st.

Shamrocks are believed to have roots which demonstrate a spiritual ministry. Amazingly, four leaf clovers are identified as providing abundant good fortune to a person. The ancient Celtic religion and others have recognized the three-leaved shamrock as a sacred plant as the number three (3) is viewed as a mystical number. St. Patrick used the shamrock to illustrate God as the Father, Son and Holy Spirit. March 17 is St. Patrick's Day, which is the date St. Patrick died and is a holiday which celebrates Ireland both religiously and culturally.

The color green signifies a spring season and new growth. Clover leaves of shamrocks can be green or red, although I've never seen a red clover. Green is frequently referred to as a healing color. When I researched chakras, our body's energy points, the fourth chakra is an emerald color located in the center of our body, which is called a heart chakra. Unconditional love is present in the heart chakra which provides guidance and supports us through the most difficult times. The heart chakra symbolizes a harmonic relationship between our body and spirit and an ability to heal ourselves and others.

When I look at one leaf of a clover, I visualize the shape of a heart. Throughout history a shamrock has provided so much healing in such a beautiful way. Many believe that the beautiful green color of the shamrock represents one's new birth and eternal life. When I look at each cluster of three leaves that are designed together, I see an incredible picture of an angel. I love the lyrics in the song "When Irish Eyes Are Smiling." "In the lilt of Irish laughter you can hear the angels sing." Archangel Raphael, the chief healing angel, is always shown wearing a bright color green (*Archangels and Ascended Masters*, Doreen Virtue, PhD).

My parents have a black plastic compost barrel in their backyard that lies next to one white-flowered lilac bush. The remaining lilac bushes produce purple flowers. They educated me that compost barrel is filled with their fruits and vegetable scraps, which are later used for fertilizing flowering and vegetable plants. Every spring, Dad takes a barrel full of the compost to place on new flowering plants around the house and the rest he places in the garage. The compost pile was protected from extreme cold and came alive in the springtime. In May of 2009, one year after my accident, my dad headed to the garage to nestle bird seed for their lovely birds. As he walked into the garage, he noticed two stems sticking out of the compost each bearing a single shamrock. The stems were about three inches tall and were side by side. Dad was elated and told Mom to come quickly so that she could see the shamrocks. He took their growth as a message from God symbolizing hope for him during tough times. Mom agreed that God was sending them a miraculous gift—a message that God gives us sweet surprises to boost our spirits after a difficult time.

Shamrocks were never seen in my parents' yard in Dubuque, Iowa. Shamrocks are generally purchased in flower shops near St. Patrick's Day. They mainly grow outside in Ireland where freezing temperatures do not exist. The average temperature in Ireland during January is 40 degree Fahrenheit. Horticulturists state that a shamrock or wild wood sorrel dug from outside will often not grow as a houseplant.

Mom transplanted the two shamrocks into a flower pot with her native belief in true growth and abundance of anything. Within two years of this powerful experience, the shamrocks flourished and again Mom transplanted them into a larger pot. Dad feels the beauty and growth of the shamrock displayed my continued healing journey and also represented the beauty in the relationship between Mom and me. The continuous support available from God surrounds us every day. We are truly blessed.

One wonderful fall day, mom surprised me with a gift—an Irish shamrock with three green clovers and stunning white flowers which she and Dad grew from the compost. At the monastery, I received further education, guidance and affirmations. Father Xavier stated, "Bridgid, you are a beautiful child of God." Wow, was I amazed. My experience positively impacted the struggles that existed within my spirit. It brought tears to my eyes remembering the story behind the shamrock plant, and how it had impacted our family during our challenging life journey.

In a dreadfully cold winter in 2014, my spirit withered as I witnessed the green clovers begin to turn dark brown and white flowers weren't returning. I worried when the leaves started to fall which symbolized to me that the shamrock was deteriorating. Watering once a week did not deter its struggles. Dreadful winters with limited sunshine and freezing temperatures keep me from spending time outdoors. This alters my spirit and depression re-blooms. When clover leaves begin to die, the potted shamrock plant is demonstrating that it needs a time of darkness to rest. Mom shared with me that during the period of dormancy, I need to limit watering and hold off on fertilizing the shamrock. Mom understands the process involved in moving from darkness to light. Again, my mother instinctively nurtured me through my fear, depression and sense of hopelessness through understanding the needs of a shamrock to foster it's ability to bloom and thrive again. New clover shoots do appear when the dormancy subsides. During this time period, shamrock houseplants should be near a sunny window or another area of bright light. Believe it or not, another mystical experience occurred as the shamrock returned with bright beautiful green cloves and white flowers bloomed by St. Patrick's Day! The shamrock continues to thrive with stunning white flowers in a large beautiful blue and pink designed flower pot.

CHAPTER 18

Beyond Traditional Therapies: Alternatives That Work

I participated fully in traditional therapies such as physical, occupational, and speech therapy following my accident and will always be grateful for the part they played in my recovery. But I wanted to accelerate my progress by augmenting these therapies with other less traditional alternatives. I found the following to be helpful to me.

Reiki: Healing Touch

Reiki (RAY-key), a spiritual practice was developed in Japan in the 1800s by Dr. Mikao Usui, a Buddhist, and brought to the United States in the mid-1900s by Hawayo Takata. The word *Reiki* translates as "God Light Energy" in Japanese.

The two portions of the word Reiki identify that *Rei* means "God's Wisdom or the Higher Power" and *Ki* means "life force energy." Reiki is viewed as "spiritually guided life force energy." Therefore, Reiki is a form of alternative medicine and the art of healing touch. Reiki is practiced by the simple process of laying-on of hands to channel energy from the practitioner to the patient. The Reiki ministry was delivered to me both during my hospitalizations and then years afterwards from so many wonderful healing people.

While working on my master's degree in Science, I was taught Healing Touch (HT), a technique similar to Reiki. One day all students were invited to receive healing touch from faculty if they so wished. I observed healing touch being given to a graduate student with a migraine headache, something that occurred frequently. At the completion of her healing touch she arose from the bed and I witnessed the woman's glorious smile and relaxed appearance. Her migraine headache had disappeared from her brain in such a simple short non-traumatizing procedure. Healing Touch (HT) was developed in 1989 by Janet Mentgen, RN, and the American Holistic Nurses Association (AHNA). HT is endorsed by the American Holistic Nurses Association and recognized by the National Hospice and Palliative Care Organization.

Healing touch is energy therapy which is heart-centered and produces well-being and healing of one's physical, mental, emotional and spiritual needs. This type of healing can be provided by anyone who embraces broad mindedness and believes in nurturing warm hearted care of others. Healing touch focuses on balancing and clearing the body's energy field using minimal or no physical touch as the hands are above the body. The focus involves determining if any of the body's energy field is sluggish or not rippling as it should. The ideal objective of healing touch is to remove all energetic interference to support the healing process.

In the fall of 1998, my dear friend Tammie Tomash called me with a tone of voice that displayed fear and sadness. I met Tammie when we were in college at Mount Mercy. She had an incredible spirit of joy, laughter, and determination. I loved being such a close friend of hers. Tammie was pregnant with her second child. Unfortunately, one summer day in July she began to experience horrible abdominal pain. Since she was roughly about twelve to fourteen weeks pregnant, Tammie assumed she was having a miscarriage, but the ultrasound didn't agree. The tremendous pain continued yet no miscarriage occurred. Later on, an ultrasound showed a small fibroid tumor. On many occasions, she traveled in and out of a hospital unsure of what the future of this pregnancy entailed. Tammie was restricted to bed rest and given morphine for the pain. In my experience, bed rest is a huge challenge and often despairing, especially for a mother with other children. Tammie was not allowed to return to her employment as a fabulous first grade teacher. I know now from my own experiences how she must have been feeling when so much of her previous role in life had been taken away.

During my first pregnancy with Meghan, I began feeling questionable abdominal spasms about a month before she was due. I was clueless as to the reason and cause for this discomfort. In utter shock, I learned that I was in preterm labor and thus placed on bed rest. At that time, I was working both at the University of Iowa College of Nursing as a clinical nursing instructor and caring for acutely ill pediatric patients at the UIHC. My supervisor at the College of Nursing was not pleased when I reported my need for bed rest to further maintain my pregnancy. Therefore, to commit to my role as an educator, I invited students to come to my home and I lectured to them while lying on my couch. I successfully gave birth once I was nine months pregnant and the nursing students completed their initial pediatric inpatient experience. Thank God!

Despite the episodes I experienced in my pregnancies, they didn't compare to the challenging and disheartening aspects of Tammie's. As the weeks of her continued pregnancy went by, that dreadful fibroid tumor enmeshed within her uterus and enlarged to the size and shape of an orange. A smaller fibroid tumor also began to grow within her uterus. In spite of this, no matter how large a fibroid tumor materializes, they are usually benign and rarely cause complications during pregnancy. Thank God. In addition, the fetus acquired what was presumed to be a cyst within his brain. Further fear and sadness erupted as the fetus was not growing in the standard neonatal rate of development. Around the September time frame, a further concern presented itself as the obstetrician told her that there was a strong possibility of the baby being born with Trisomy 18. Trisomy 18 is also called Edward's Syndrome. In the United States, Trisomy 18 occurs in about one of every 2,500 pregnancies. When a fetus is full term, 50 percent are stillborn. The rate of being stillborn is higher in boys than girls. Babies born with Trisomy 18 often experience significant complications within the early months and years of their life. Some of the many defects may impact the heart, kidney, stomach, intestines, brain, orthopedic, and cognitive impairment. The obstetrician told her that, if she had a live birth, her baby would probably only live one day or perhaps up to one year and with significant disabilities. He suggested that she have an abortion.

Tammie was furious—not only because of the callous manner the obstetrician delivered his prognosis but also because he encouraged her to have an abortion. Maternal blood screening can also be used but does not reveal an absolute diagnosis of Trisomy 18. Tammie didn't want extensive blood testing. That would merely enhance her stress. Blood testing during pregnancy as well as an ultrasound does not give an accurate basis of labeling something that is completely unidentifiable.

Tammie was never going to proceed with an abortion. She believed in miracles and that it was not God's intention for her baby to be born with this condition. Wonderful divine opportunities arose when she chose to leave her obstetrician and transferred her care to the University of Iowa Hospitals and Clinics for more comprehensive maternal health care. She knew that these obstetricians were very skilled in all aspects of care during pregnancy, especially complications. Tammie's faith reemerged as her new obstetrician was far more positive and didn't discuss the prevalence of Trisomy 18. Tammie was seen weekly at the University of Iowa and was closely monitored with numerous ultrasounds.

Within the fall time frame, Tammie called me and asked if I would visit her. I find it so powerfully encouraging when someone hurting asks for a friend's companionship. Tammie shared with me the tremendous heart-wrenching pregnancy she was experiencing; my mouth hung open in shock and tears fell down my face. I felt heartbroken but honored that she wanted me to come visit. While in the van, driving to visit Tammie, I thought about her uterine tumors, the possibility of Trisomy 18 and the potential outcomes.

In the midst of my fear, a message came within my spirit to remind me that I was trained and very capable of providing Tammie with Healing Touch which is non- invasive. I prayed to God and the angels for divine guidance and support in my efforts to help Tammie and her baby begin their healing process. When I gently explained to Tammie what healing touch is, I could sense by the look on her face that she was a bit shocked. Tammie had only asked me to visit her not expecting anything further, especially healing touch. Tammie had never heard of healing touch. But she smiled and was comfortable allowing me to proceed.

In administering healing touch, the individual is in a comfortable position, lying down on his/her back on a bed or table. I began the process at Tammie's feet where my hands are raised two to three inches above her body without actually touching her. I proceeded all the way up to her head and asked those angels for guidance and healing as this is so beyond my natural abilities. A very strong sensation of heat arises from any area, when a change appears to be occurring. When I approached Tammie's abdominal area, I could feel a very large circular area that was sending intense heat toward my hands from the right and a smaller area on the left. Although I was unaware, these were the areas in which the fibroid tumors were located. When I detected these areas, my hands circled around the affected area.

I began asking the Divine to heal Tammie and her baby as the negative energy released and pulled out of her body and towards the windows that were near her. When I finished, I sent continued divine healing from heaven that soared through my hands. The intense heat that I had felt earlier had disappeared. I smiled and thanked God for helping me provide healing touch. I completed by sending Tammie's body such love, peace and serenity. When Tammie opened her eyes, she preciously smiled at me and shared the incredible relaxation that emerged. Her abdominal pain was reduced significantly and she was now able to easily fall asleep.

A few days later, Tammie visited her obstetrician and again received another ultrasound. The obstetrician was utterly shocked as he saw in amazement that Tammie's largest fibroid tumor had significantly decreased in size! His mouth opened as he was stunned and questioned how on earth this occurred. He asked Tammie if she received any other type of treatment available to reduce the fibroid tumors. Tammie was uncomfortable sharing that she received healing touch from her friend who is a nurse. Internally, I was frightened for Tammie to share this as well. I assumed that her obstetrician or any physician would find alternative medicine very questionable, especially during that time period. Utilizing Eastern medicine was a fairly new way of providing healing care in contrast to Western medicine. Tammie's pregnancy greatly improved because she was largely pain free and was able to resume part-time teaching during October to December. Jordon was born on December 30, miraculously healthy at thirty-four weeks' gestation despite being due on February 9.

Tammie shared that she was grateful that I, whom she felt was a special, loving, and caring friend, took the time to support and further heal her and Jordon. In my mind, God moved through me to enhance the healing process. Another profound miracle identified its presence in my life, one that I will never forget. There is no harm in providing healing touch to anyone suffering. Today, I find it fascinating that I know of a surgeon who provides healing touch as she operates on patients. Eastern and alternative medicine provides relevant opportunities to help heal those who are suffering. I have utilized healing touch for relief from headaches, tendon, muscular and bone pain. Ryan has always told me when he is in pain and knows how I will assist in healing it. I continue to administer healing touch to any member of my family who asks, despite my teenagers looking at me oddly.

Mindfulness Meditation

Over time I have learned that mindfulness meditation is an incredible way to relax, let go, and receive simple messages given to our true self. Mindfulness meditation trains us to focus on the present and abandon all the worries about the past or future that bog us down. Cortisone, our stress hormone, is highly decreased even through a very simple meditation. I used to believe that to properly meditate, I was required to use some sort of detailed or guided meditation which should take a certain amount of time for its effectiveness. A *Frontiers in Human Neuroscience* article remarks that portions of our brain's realm responds when emotional energy is altered through meditation which can also occur when a person isn't actively meditating. True simplicity in meditation is a fabulous way to reduce our stress and change our physiological, emotional and spiritual environment. I love witnessing how quickly my blood pressure and heart rate reduce, following simple slow, deep breathing and allowing my tight muscles to relax. I didn't know until recently how often my muscles are tense, even upon awakening.

The most efficient way to do mindfulness meditation is to let go of my control of my day's activities and visualize simplicity. I've noticed at night when I'm trying to sleep I intuitively breathe slowly in and out each for the count of ten. I reflect on all that I was grateful to God for that day, even the beautiful sunshine. I also think about what occurred during the day that I need to change or improve on either emotionally or behaviorally. I then gently tap the right side of my upper back as if I'm a baby. Finally, I gently sway side to side, as if I'm being rocked in a rocking chair. Both are ways that I communicate with my body to let go and rest as if I'm an infant needing consoling and peace.

Healing Amenities of Exercise

I value exercise as an incredible process to restore and revitalize one's mind, body and physical health. Around the time of my discharge from the hospital, I weighed one hundred and ten pounds. My weight has increased to normalcy yet I note that I still eat slowly, as if I'm back in time re-learning how to eat solid food. Within the first six months of outpatient rehabilitation, I really wanted to resume my athletic activities, especially since I was preparing for my first triathlon before the accident. I questioned my ability to effectively return to weight lifting. I asked my outpatient occupational therapist if he would train me in lifting weights again. No, I didn't think at all about being so thin, having a broken right collar bone, poor balance, cervical fracture or a collapsed lung. His eyes and mouth opened wide, as if in shock at my question. He smiled somewhat and stared at me as if he were surprised by my goals and determination. This occupational therapist was working with me on relearning how to play simple games. I often cried about my lost ability to play games. Internally, I knew that exercise would promote my sense of self-worth and enhance a higher belief in my abilities.

Exercising boosts my mind, body and spirit and thus highlights the forthcoming day, as I am a morning exerciser. If I feel anxiety, fear, sadness or anger before I exercise, it reduces significantly after I get started. My external picture of myself is reflected through my grateful smile. Internally my inner spirit blossoms into such gratitude and my heart bursts with such joy. There is no harm in exercising effectively, although I can overindulge in my routine and may not pay attention to the message my brain and physiological body are communicating within me. Symptoms that I've experienced could be tendon or muscle pain and/or light-headedness, as if my blood sugar was beginning to drop. Today when such feelings emerge within me, I've learned to pay attention and embrace the message given to me. I must stop what I'm doing and work on true healing. Despite this, my determination continues to thrive. Today, I am mesmerized by the tremendous progress I have achieved in strength training. Before the accident, I was never able or truly willing to advance in neither further types of strength training nor further sets of reputation. Todd encouraged me to do more repetitions and slowly increase the weight. I proceeded to doing four repetitions with sets of 15-20. Prior to the accident I did three repetitions with 12-15 sets. Perhaps my aging into the 50's with numerous mental and physical altering changes propels me even further. Therefore, a very powerful trigger is mindfulness, something I'm continuing to learn, embrace, and honor the meanings placed in my life's journey.

The Healing Dynamics of Laughter and Yoga

The Free Dictionary defines yoga as "an ascetic Hindu discipline involving controlled breathing, prescribed body positions, and meditation, with the goal of attaining a state of deep spiritual insight and tranquility." I restarted using beginner's yoga, to keep the exercise simple. I am blown away by the peace and relaxation that I feel. I find it very powerful what Buddha states: "The mind is everything. What you think you become." As you finish the class you hold your hands when sitting and bend over with your eyes closed and say "Namaste." The meaning of this word says to me: "The spirit within me honors the spirit with you." Namaste is an incredible way to send others such passion and reassurance for their life's experience. As I leave the class I sway gently with a smile.

"Laughter is sacred. Laugh more, play more, and sing more to harmonize with you the natural world. Nirvana is joy and carefree laughter. Laughter truly is the best medicine of all--you take yourself far too seriously and in so doing, you edge out the secret of harmony on your planet: living in joy. Today, seek out ten people who are not smiling, and go out of your way to put a smile on their face. In that way, you will have lit ten candles of light amid darkness." (Doreen Virture, PhD)

I struggled relearning how to laugh. I questioned its true existence. Despite misery, my brain waves erupted about two years after the accident. Laughter truly resumed when I was watching a hilarious movie with Ryan. He had such a surprised look on his face and then a smile burst through. I was so enlightened and thrilled this occurred and the laughter didn't end. I'm not the only one who laughs hearing the dynamics of the humor in my recovery. Everyone who listens busts their gut! Laughter demonstrates mental and physical prosperity.

My precious mother, despite the tragedy she was experiencing, shared hilarious information during a visit from Dr. Jane Bourgeois, a woman so dear to me. She is a chiropractor and healing arts professional- bringing science and healing energy together, awakening the field of energy that surrounds each and every one of us. Her business is entitled, Synchronicity. In the 1920s, Carl Jung, MD, a Swiss psychologist, defined synchronicity, per Wikipedia, as "the occurrence of two or more events that appear to be meaningfully related but not causally related." Synchronicity holds that such events are "meaningful coincidences." I find this to be such a divine description of synchronicity, which I well understand. I have seen Dr. Jane for so many years. She has healed my neck, back, right clavicle, arm trauma and migraines.

Dr. Jane came to my bedside when I was hospitalized providing holistic healing touch and administering essential oils to me. Norene, my mother in law, was observing her with intrigue and asked mom what her name was and her area of specialty. In mom's fatigue, she replied, "That is Dr. Jane." Norene replied, "What is her specialty?" Mom replied, "Dr. Jane is a veterinarian." Norene looked at Mom with such a confused state of mind and questioned its reality. This wonderful story continues to make everyone burst into laughter when Mom shares one of her hilarious healing adventures.

Norene gave Mom some beautiful pink summer pajamas that were Capri in length. She knew mom slept with me in my hospital room. Mom loved those pajamas especially since they looked so sleek and stylish. Since it was summer time, Mom wore them not only in my bedroom but also to, from and within the hospital! She felt as if the pajamas looked like a regular outfit. Mom continues to wear those pajamas as an adorable summer outfit, which many find hysterical!

My sister Kathleen walked into the hospital wearing my fluffy cotton pink robe, despite it being May! She loved how it felt as it provided her with comfort and nurturing when coming to visit me, especially when I was in a coma. Kathleen adored the robe so much that she even wore it walking into the hospital for lunch! I wonder if others chuckled when they saw her wearing a robe in the summer surrounded by so many people. One day after eating lunch she returned to the ICU and placed the robe directly on me. Powerfully, her purpose was to make me feel like I was home again.

Laughter Yoga

I had never heard of laughter yoga before. As time progressed, I began to find humor in movies, things my family shared, and things I said and did. But, I hadn't gotten to the point that I could truly let go and *really* laugh. The practice of laughter yoga includes prolonging voluntary laughter until it becomes real laughter. It is easily transported when utilized with a group of people who aren't afraid to be playful. I discovered further insight on the website www.laughteryoga.org. Bangalore, India, researched laughter yoga and found that it strengthens the immune system. Our overall stress hormones and blood pressure are reduced. People immediately become linked in with others and relationships build. After your first experience, laughter easily becomes an embraced part of one's life.

I first tried laughter yoga taught online through a podcast by a teacher, Patrick Sterenchuk. I was unable to see him, but through his instruction, started gently laughing right away, without him stating anything funny. I eventually laughed so long and hard it concerned my children. They had such a bewildered and mad look on their faces stating, "Mom, what's wrong with you?" I loved their reaction as this was an indication of why I continued laughing in my healing journey.

While viewing the schedule of speakers at the Brain Injury Alliance of Iowa's annual conference, which I attend yearly, I was delighted to read that laughter yoga was going to be presented by a man named Mike Lewis. Mike is a traumatic brain injury survivor who is employed at On with Life in Ankeny, Iowa. On with Life is a nonprofit organization and a Midwest leader in post acute inpatient and outpatient brain injury rehabilitation as well as independent living. Since 1991, On with Life has served 2,500 brain injury survivors and their families.

Mike has impacted and thus enhanced the recovery of those with brain injury through using laughter yoga. Patients have gone near him in a wheel chair laughing remarkably when they visualize him. Both I and anyone who knows Mike adore him for all the amazing healing gifts he provides us. Mike has generously educated me on the prolonged value of nurturing yourself with laughter, despite life's struggles.

Biking

One of the greatest joys I have experienced was when I climbed up on my mountain bike for the first time since my accident. I began to gently ride on a short simple trail with Todd and Ryan, eleven months after the accident. Memories of how to get on a bike, where to travel on a trail, put on a helmet and stop when necessary gradually came back to me slowly but surely. A natural high embraced within me despite feeling somewhat nervous, as I pedaled along a flat trail on a beautiful warm spring day for the first time! No fear continued to exist within me in spite of me knowing Ryan rode close next to me. His face had such a cautious look on it. Ryan and my other children had witnessed so much tragedy; but I delivered them a message that, despite their fear, I was never going to quit riding a bike. Since my accident, many friends have shared their fears of never wanting to return to ride a bike again. This brings such sadness to my heart. Never quit!

On the one year anniversary of my accident, I arose at five a.m. with feelings of such despair as I recalled the many unintended alterations in my life. Stamina returned, however, and gave me the idea to return to my bike and pedal the entire trail that I pursued before my accident. Since it was early in the morning and Todd was out of town, I didn't ask anyone to join me. In reality, I wanted to bike alone, in my own space and time. Not knowing the potential implications, I called by dear friend Amy. I left a message on her cell phone describing where I was headed and how much I cared for her.

My sister-in-law, Val, called me from Rochester, Minnesota, questioning how I was doing. Val is a registered nurse at Mayo Clinic. I told her I was preparing to ride on the bike trail again by myself. Val was utterly shocked stating, "What are you thinking, Bridgid?" Her voice shuddered. She encouraged me to wear my helmet, take a cell phone and call her once I finished going down and up that hill that was filled with mud last year. Angie and I never took cell phones when we rode. But this time I agreed to take mine, although part of me thought, *Oh, Val, if the same type of accident reoccurs, I won't be coherent enough to utilize a cell phone.*

Internally, my intermittent fear left and I jumped on one of our mountain bikes. I talked to those incredible angels before I started to put on my helmet and continued praying as I peddled away from home. Tennis shoes were on, not biking shoes. After I crossed railroad tracks, the hill emerged. A tiny fear arose. I encouraged my spirit to let it go and continue pedaling. I rode at a simple speed with both arms firmly holding the grips. With utter determination I pedaled down that hill where no mud or water appeared at the base. I pedaled upward with such enthusiasm. I made it to the top of the trail and let out a loud cry. This cry wasn't sadness it was the experience of utter JOY! I made it through that 11 mile trail with such success. I called Val when I arrived onto a flat part of the trail. I was so grateful and honored that oh yes I can move forward above and beyond my previous life's experience!

I have no fear riding my bike now, especially alone on a trail. At times, when walkers or bikers emerge a sense of fear arises. Therefore, I deep breathe and say to myself, "*Oh, yes, you can.*" Alone time is very crucial for me as it instills peace, joy, determination, and gratitude which further guides me forward on my healing journey. I went to one of the most beautiful bluff regions in Decorah, Iowa. An eleven-mile loop trail, entitled Trout Run, journeys you through numerous vibrant cliffs. The trail is used for hiking, cross country skiing, walking, biking and horse riding. It is surrounded by incredible bluffs that weave through bow string bridges, parks, farmland, trout stream and Upper Iowa River, and amazing wildlife. Many folks wonder and verbalize, "Is this heaven?" Feeling naturally high riding this trail, I embrace my ability to successfully soar through the entirety of its challenges!

Decorah has incredible trout fishing opportunities along Trout Trail. Todd, Ryan, and Grandpa Ruden are incredible trout fishermen and frequently travel up north to various streams, every weekend if their schedule allowed. The trout stream is spring fed. The bald eagles' home base is located across the street from a trout hatchery. The most incredible wildlife that I see frequently is the bald eagles. Decorah Eagle Cam Alert is a detailed account of numerous residing bald eagles which demonstrates their birth and further growth through the years.

Bald eagles nests are the largest of all birds and are five to six feet in diameter and three feet tall. The display of the nests and the bald eagles themselves electrify my spirit as my eyes and mouth open in such astonishment, especially when I visualize them when I'm biking, walking, kayaking, jogging, or canoeing. Eagles fly higher than any other bird. And in their radiant soar to the sky, people will instinctively drift by in time to observe them. Witnessing their presence as I bike ride through the beautiful trail, I am enlightened with such peace, joy, and reflection of all for which I am so grateful.

A rest stop provides numerous posters with pictures and documentation describing the lifestyle of the bald eagles. I wanted to learn more, but my reading difficulties continue to challenge me. My attention and desire to read one or two paragraphs of a poster is a slow process. My brain is overstimulated to read, understand, and remember the words. Therefore, these aspects reduce my desire or interest in reading any further. I do remember reading about the impact a huge number of awful biting gnats produced earlier this summer. They horribly bit the eagles in so many places which caused red raised itchy painful skin. On a poster, a picture was shown of numerous gnats circling around eagles resting in their nest. I was so saddened that several of the young eagles died following their exposure to such destructive bugs. This symbolizes another aspect of life over which we have no control. We'll see what happens this summer. More miracles could bring further blessings.

Nutrition

The benefit of incorporating healthy nutrients into our body intrigues me. About six months after my accident, I started craving dark green vegetables especially broccoli along with salmon. I couldn't understand this craving in any way, shape or form; thus I consulted my physician. He smiled and encouraged me to contact Dr. Terry Wahls, a clinical professor of medicine at the University of Iowa Carver College of Medicine and staff physician at the Veterans Hospital. Terry teaches internal medicine to medical stu-

dents and resident physicians and sees patients with traumatic brain injury and complex chronic health problems.

When Terry began her position of the University
of Iowa in 2000, she was unfortunately diagnosed with
degenerative multiple sclerosis (MS). Her MS symptoms
started to very slowly cause her to deteriorate. By 2003,
despite chemotherapy to reduce the flow of the disease,
she required a wheel chair. She feared becoming bed rid-
den and thus began researching vitamins and supplements
for progressive brain disorders instead of investigating
all the drugs that were years away from FDA approval.
Through her research she determined which valuable nutrients were critical to be consumed for brain growth.

Terry decided to supplement her diet with vitamin-en-
riched foods and encouraged physical therapists to provide
her with neurological electrical stimulation. In one year,
Terry no longer needed a wheelchair or a cane and slowly
began to walk even more effectively. She was able to resume
her bike riding and rode an 18-mile bicycle tour in one
day! The power of functional medicine and lifestyle change
enhances all who suffer from any chronic auto immune condition. To improve the altered condition of the brain, Dr.
Wahls recommends nine cups per day of dark green vegetables and fruit. In addition, exercise one hour per day six
days a week. For further information, consult Terry's website
at www.terrywahls.com or her book, *The Wahls Protocol.*

As I've looked into the value of sufficient nutrition, I
have learned a great deal about the power of utilizing antioxidants in our diet. Antioxidants diminish the impact of
free radicals which unfortunately deteriorate body cells.
Those nasty free radicals, a molecule enclosed with at least
one unpaired electron, can easily damage tissues. Our earth
provides us with so many healing elements easily acquired

at a low cost to enhance our overall health. The simplistic antioxidants are vegetables, fruits, whole grains, nuts and legumes. I find it fascinating that I continue to crave foods loaded with antioxidants. For instance, to name a few of the fruits and vegetables that my brain and body cry out for include dark green lettuce, pea pods, avocado, broccoli, chickpeas, bell peppers, berries, raisins, prunes, dates, and grapes. I also crave almonds, cashews, pecans and whole grain breads and cereal and legumes such as black beans.

To my astonishment, I learned that the oil in cold water fish is filled with omega-3 fatty acids. These are healthy fats that can boost a crucial portion of our brain's capability to heighten more normal function. I continue to crave salmon but I also love eating fresh trout, sea bass and halibut. The foods I crave are sent as a messenger from my brain. This ignites a power within to attract my attention to seek particular food to enhance my healing.

Interestingly enough, Todd, Ryan, and Grandpa Ruden love to head north to capture trout. They search for a secluded, undisturbed area. They cast out their fishing lure into a clear stream. I love witnessing their glowing smiles that emerge when the trout swims directly toward their brightly colored lure, and bites on. To the trout's dismay, it's pulled inward with a circling reel to land in the trout fisherman's hands. Todd prepares trout in such a fabulous homemade recipe that even the kids love! Again a dynamic healing is provided when you eat a fresh fish.

Initially, I was overwhelmed by the idea of maintaining my diet loaded in fruits and vegetables. Over time, I craved eating the vegetables even more and gradually learned how to add fruits in my daily diet, something I've never done before. I add fresh fruit such as a combination of blueberries, bananas, raspberries, and blackberries to my fiber and whole grain cereal. In order to have a sufficient diet, I also take a liquid dietary supplement enriched with whole foods which are filled with vitamins, minerals, and amino acids. In addition, I add fish oil, which also contains omega-3 fatty acids in an appropriate amount. Both fish oil and omega-3 fatty acids improve many health-related conditions and interestingly are perceived as a brain nurturing food. Red wine was okay but only one glass per day, as increased amounts alter effectiveness of my seizure medication. I loved red wine but craved it too much, another disease from which I needed recovery. I have learned that alcohol is not a successful medication necessary to reduce suffering, fear, anger, depression and bewilderment. Alcohol abuse only makes the severity of such emotions more profound.

Acupuncture

During my earthly voyage, my mind, body, and spirit explored various paradigms that embraced the ultimate healing. This is uniquely existent between the medical disciplines of Eastern, Western, and alternative care. I have already shared the stunning and curing encounters I've had with healing related to prayer, angels, Reiki/healing touch, and embracing signs sent from God. But there is more for me to share.

Unfortunately, my worst grand mal seizure affected several regions of my brain and took away my ability to breathe and thus absorb oxygen. This seizure occurred when Molly and I were lying on my bed watching TV. I had slept sufficiently that day. We were going to Ryan's junior high football game when all of a sudden I said to Molly, "I don't feel so good." I then began to have a grand mal seizure. Molly was only nine-years-old but knew to call 911. How terrifying it must feel to witness your parent unconscious and seizing uncontrollably. This is such a devastating experience for anyone to witness. All of my children have witnessed my grand mal seizures but never Todd. Regrettably, as I was taken in an ambulance to the hospital, I quit breathing.

With my loss of such valuable oxygen, I was placed on a ventilator, or breathing machine, during my hospitalization. When I awoke and seemed more alert and neurologically intact, they removed the breathing tube. As I began to walk from the bed to the bathroom, I had numbness, tingling, and weakness all the way down my left leg. I was confused and questioned its reality of existence. When a neurologist saw me the next morning, I shared the symptoms in my left leg and asked, "Have I had the beginning of a stroke"? She appeared in a hurry to get her rounds done and said, "No, it's just neurological." Nothing more was said. This made no sense to me. I wanted her to define "neurological" in addition to explaining why on earth I would have difficulty walking.

A physical therapist with a dull, tired look on his face walked with me. He asked, "So you want to go home with a cane?" Annoyed, I said "no", having no idea what the future would hold for me. Would my previous walking capacity never return? Was it forever? Unfortunately, I did not receive further information and was discharged. I received no resources for future physical therapy or any future follow-up! In my mind, this is an inappropriate way to administer health care.

The numbness, tingling, and weakness in my entire left leg continued. The cells within my brain soar in oblivion. For a month, I could barely walk sufficiently and fell several times. My frustration escalated since I received no effective treatment for this condition from Western medicine. My sister-in-law, Lori, suggested that I should consider acupuncture.

Acupuncture is a traditional Chinese medicine, which some describe as alternative medicine, created in China before 2500 BC to heal disease and reduce pain. The Chinese believe that good health is based on a balance between the yin and yang—the paradoxical forces within us that are reciprocal. When the yin and yang become unequal and unbalanced, the body begins to malfunction. Therefore, tiny metal needles are gently inserted into the flow and passageway of the body's vital energy to restore and balance the yin and yang, of their neurological disabilities.

I was, of course, frightened to think about having needles stuck in my body. But after researching the benefits of acupuncture and suffering for such a long time, I decided to try Eastern medicine and Todd was in agreement. We discovered Dr. Yang Ahn, a physician who began offering acupuncture to his family practice patients who suffered from low back pain and headaches. Seeing positive results with those patients, he expanded the practice to treat a variety of health concerns with acupuncture. Dr. Ahn provides acupuncture to those suffering from brain injury or stroke. In his experience, when merely utilizing Western medicine, there is no practical way to stimulate our neurologic system to heal.

My acupuncturist, Dr. Ahn, listened to me describe my experience before, during and after the seizure and then watched me walk. When I shared the dynamics of my grand mal seizure, Dr. Ahn stated, "Bridgid, this is the beginning of a stroke because you had no oxygen to your brain when you quit breathing during the seizure." I was stunned yet grateful that my presumption that it might be a stroke wasn't ludicrous. I saw Dr. Ahn once a week for one month. My numbness, tingling, and weakness decreased down my leg each week until it was gone. I smiled and hugged Dr. Ahn with such gratitude, as I do anyone who helps me heal. Hugs

I give to others have always been an important necessity in my life. My mother recently shared what the letters in the word "Hugs" represents. H is-help. U is-us. G is-grow. S is-spiritually. Help us grow spiritually. A divine and powerful message that emerges to the one who receives a simple hug.

Dr. Ahn has repeatedly witnessed the incredible value of acupuncture as it stimulates our brain to heal rapidly—faster and far more thoroughly than Western medicine. Traumatic brain injury and stroke patients truly witness the significant improvement of their neurologic disabilities. Acupuncture is so simple yet often overlooked as a valuable treatment for numerous health conditions. It is extremely cost effective and, most importantly, provides incredible healing outcomes without any side effects.

The Essence of Art Therapy

I attend an epilepsy support group provided by the Epilepsy Foundation of Iowa. I was asked to be involved with an art class that they were offering. I was shocked as I'm not an artist. I questioned what is art therapy? Once again despite my life's alterations, I am continuing to learn so much about the valuable therapy that I never knew even existed. In the 1940s, mental health care professionals initiated art therapy (www.arttherapy.org). Art therapy strengthens mental, emotional, and even physiological conditions. Therapists utilize art media in an innovative way to examine one's conflicts in their life. Some of its impacts include self-awareness, behavior management, social skills, reduces anxiety and addiction, and increases self-esteem. Visual art is utilized such as painting, drawing, sculpture and other forms.

The Brain Injury Alliance of Colorado (BIAC) conveys the following benefit of art therapy for people with brain injuries:

- Improves focus, stamina, fine motor skills, cognitive functioning, problem solving ability, and coping skills
- Provides another means of communication and increases verbalization
- Provides a means of addressing social and emotional difficulties related to disability, trauma, and loss
- Provides a means of exploring changes to identity and self-image
- Improves self-esteem and confidence
- Decreases depression and anxiety
- Improves quality of life

The BIAC provides a six-week Art Therapy Process Group led by Nancy Kelley Franke, MA, LPC, ATR. The art therapy group focuses on the impacts brain injury has to a survivor's self-image. Students are encouraged to share their grief, identification of the power within them, belief in their future goals which are provided by a supportive community.

The most powerful example of the gift available within art is displayed on www.btizzy.com. This is a free online marketplace connecting people with disabilities to consumers and employers. The founder of Out of Step is Nikki Zimmerman, a mother of a child with disabilities. One story on the website illustrates a man with cerebral palsy who is significantly disabled. He demonstrates his ability to beautifully paint a strikingly brilliant wall in a home! This brought tears to my ears as he demonstrates the dynamics within disabilities.

I was shown the art work displayed by those in the art class for those with epilepsy. The artistry was so beautiful and touching as they wrote the emotions they felt and why they painted what they did. So many are not artists by profession! The art therapy counselor shared that the children she works with at the University of Iowa Children's Hospital respond to art therapy as they move from challenging emotions and behavior to a more peaceful state, even a three-year-old! I attended an amazing Wisconsin Brain Injury Conference entitled Mind, Body, and Spirit in Brain Injury. An art therapist showed the artistry of those with brain injury. One woman who was hospitalized painted on the wall in her hospital room! Her negative emotional behavior changed dramatically after completing her drawings. Survivors are the ones who have shown me the dramatic effect of incorporating artistry in treatment. Therefore, I am taking the art therapy class this spring! Such power in all that I continue to learn about ways to help me heal!

The Power of Music

Music is an incredibly beautiful art form composed of melody, rhythm and harmony. For as long as my brain recalls, music has ministered to me. Our unbelievable brain has such a magical way to create a new life trail despite areas that are injured. This process is called neuroplasticity or brain plasticity. Injury and disease alter the brain's infrastructure and create new nerve cells in the brain to compensate for such alterations. Thankfully the role of neuroplasticity is well known during the recovery from brain damage. I found it very powerful to read that Dr. Oliver Sack, a neurologist, wrote, "Nothing activates the brain so extensively as music."

When I was in second grade, I was taught to play the piano by an older Catholic nun, one who rarely smiled. Although I learned a great deal about music for the first time, I was frightened of making a mistake. She slapped my hand hard with a thin wooden ruler when I made a mistake. Fear of how I perform in any situation can be disheartening, but I have learned over time how to let it go. I continued playing the piano through high school. In the 1970s, I had an incredible teacher, who had won a beauty pageant and displayed elegance in her mannerisms. She knew how to support me, even when I made mistakes. I loved the feeling of placing my fingers on the keys to enounce a rhythm and sound of a song, especially those that moved me emotionally.

During the first year following my brain injury, I needed something to lift my spirit. I questioned my capability to resume playing the piano as I had previously done. Wouldn't my memory loss, difficult concentration, muscle spasms, and poor reading abilities take away this gift? Since I couldn't drive, a very kind piano teacher came to my home to re-educate me. I doubted myself and often cried in front of her. She gently shared with compassion the story of her husband's own life experience. Her husband was a very gifted musician who played the guitar. He unfortunately had a stroke and during recovery he questioned his return to being a musician. With perseverance, he regained his passion for music and skills as a musician and at the same level of talent he had before the stroke! I internalized his capability and the power of the brain to heal. Lo and behold, I remembered the sounds and rhythms of songs. I ventured backward in time to regain what I thought must be lost and was able to sufficiently play the piano as I had previously! Such a natural high erupted.

Music has a tremendous capability to heal. True recovery from much life altering disease is enhanced with music therapy. Our brain activity stimulates the flow of blood and oxygen with the power of music. This spring I attended the Iowa Brain Injury Association Conference. I had the privilege to hear Jason Crigler tell his story. His presentation was entitled "Defining the Odds: Reclaiming Life." Jason is a thirty-four-year-old guitarist and song writer. While Jason was playing the guitar in a show on stage, his life was completely turned upside down. Jason's blood vessel in his brain ruptured. Physicians didn't believe that he would live through the night.

Again, another miracle occurred and Jason survived. Jason needed to master every life skill, and deal with aphasia and several handicaps. Once he returned home he started trying to play the guitar. Jason was so fragile and vulnerable. He experienced pain within five to ten minutes of playing the guitar. Unbelievably, Jason wrote and sang "The Books on the Shelf" while playing the guitar. Some of the powerful words in the song include: "I lost my voice in the forest. My body was on a tight rope. What if I fall today? Stuck in the cracks and laughed." Despite all of Jason's turmoil, the lyrics show us that laughter can occur even while fastened in one of life's holes. The power of music in healing the brain is astronomical.

I never recall being aware of music therapists for both adults and children before my accident. In the hospital pediatric step-down unit, I have worked with wonderful child life therapists who sometimes utilized music in their treatment regimen. Music therapy is now more highly recognized as a health care profession and research-based discipline. Music therapy is a college education program which is board certified and can be further enhanced with a master's degree.

Music embellishes the exploration of one's self. Music therapy is identified as a pathway to improve one's physiological, cognitive, emotional and social well-being (www. musictherapy.org). It is known to decrease pain, stress, and anxiety, lower blood pressure and heart rate, improve respiration and cardiac output, and relax muscle strain. When exposed to music, patients become more alive and confident in their healing journey. The Brain Injury Alliance of Colorado offers a six week class led by music therapists. Live music, movement, and playing an instrument are utilized to address social, emotional, and speech goals. No music ability is required (www.biacolorado.org).

Music Decreases Aphasia Struggles

Aphasia does not affect our intelligence, though many think so. The most common cause of aphasia is a stroke, whereby specific regions of the brain are flawed. Further causes of aphasia include cancer, epilepsy and Alzheimer's disease. I find it fascinating that in 1871, an article written by a neurologist, Dr. John Hughlings Jackson, stated, "It has been known literally for centuries that speechless people, people who have lost speech, may sing." Music stimulates numerous coordinating entities of the left and front sides of the brain as well as the deep regions of the brain where memory and emotion are cultivated.

Music therapy benefits persons with aphasia because it strengthens breathing and verbal capacity, improves expression of speech and enhances both verbal and nonverbal communication. The techniques utilized by music therapists accentuate memory, rhythm, pitch, and vocal transformation. The effectiveness is strengthened or decreased by the music choice and the nature in how it was expressed. With aphasia, certain audiovisual structures vary greatly in speech improvement with available audio and social cues. I viewed a video of Congresswoman Gabby Gifford who sustained a brain injury from a gunshot wound to the head and is challenged by aphasia. I was surprised to hear how much more articulate she was when she was singing.

Beth Morden, a friend who is much more challenged by aphasia than I am, drove with me to an aphasia support group at the University of Iowa Wendell Johnson Speech and Hearing Clinic, where we both received speech therapy. Having suffered a severe stroke secondary to a heart tumor, Beth can only use one or two words. All the hard work that Beth does to improve her aphasia is remarkable.

My aphasia became more evident and noticeable when I was with Beth. Things that I would say could be strange and shocking at times. No, this was not purposeful. For instance, I tried to say "pencil" and said "penis." Our laughter erupted into hysteria and I nearly wet my pants! Beth, a woman with aphasia, didn't find me disgusting but understood the meaning of my words. Thank God this didn't happen to me with others on a routine basis. The most phenomenal day occurred when I asked Beth a question. She struggled with her response to me and instead sang the entire "Happy Birthday" song to me, demonstrating the power of music in stimulating the brain's enhanced function.

Delighted by Dance

Author Sherrilyn Kenyon profoundly wrote, "Life isn't finding shelter in a storm, it's about learning how to dance in the rain." Dance is a luxurious form of art which is administered through movement that enlightens the body, mind, and spirit. Dance improves health, coordination, movement, muscle tone, thinking skills, motivation, and memory. Our brain is positively stimulated from dance. It enlightens our thinking skills, motivation and memory. Dance provides us with a safe outlet for anger, frustration, and depression. Dance helps people feel joyful and confident. Today my inner spirit continues to thrive and crave the beauty of dance more than it ever has. I truly do dance in the rain!

When I was five years old, my dad introduced glorious dance into my life. As I began to receive my first dance lesson, I stood on my dad's feet holding on to his warm hands as he guided me into the movement. I tried to hold my left hand somewhere on his left arm and my right hand holding Dad's left hand in a closed position. My back, head, and arms were positioned for proper stance and posture. Peaceful waltz music was playing while Dad began teaching me ballroom box waltz. The style of the waltz dance steps illustrates the shape of a box. The lead dancer gently escorts the partner guiding her right foot to step backward; holding the step and bringing her left foot parallel to her right foot in the count of one, two, and three. Then her left foot is guided to step away to the left and drawing her right foot to connect to her left. This pattern continues on to complete the shape of a square.

Dad was delighted to witness me express such joy as my smiles never ceased. I learned to hear a rhythm and dance precisely to the beat. I remember dancing in high school during a gym class but remember feeling intimidated being with a partner I didn't know. Rhythm and blues music has thrilled me since I was young. I loved to move and groove with my cousins or good friends, especially in college. Just before Todd and I were married, I begged to learn ballroom dancing. I wanted so badly to dance well to our reception song, "Here and Now," by Luther Vandross. In my imagination, we did dance perfectly.

Fifteen years later, Todd and I returned to ballroom dancing lessons, which I begged for. The class included waltz, foxtrot, swing, and cha-cha. Dancing offered a miraculous way to boost a relationship! Swing dancing was my absolute favorite. I loved the music, the rhythm, and faster paced movement of the dance steps. My heart and spirit leapt with true joy, as I smiled all the way through the song. Todd always wanted to remain in the beginning level one class. I can appreciate now how challenging the dance leader position is since that person is responsible for control of the movements. I tried to boost Todd's spirit as I truly believed in his dancing ability. Thus, I went ahead and signed us up for a level two class. Eventually, we successfully made it to level three of the four class sessions. This was a wonderful adventure and so therapeutic to spend such wonderful quality time together. Dance and dinner were such a fabulous way to connect with each other. With our busy schedule, however, it was rare for us to truly get out and dance publically.

When Molly was in pre-school her teacher, Diana, began introducing the children to the beautiful Spanish language. One morning, I heard Latin music playing. The kids were dancing along. My eyes must have opened wide and sparkled with such a smile. Diana could tell that I loved the music and encouraged me to take a salsa dance class. Salsa is Latin American music that incorporates rhythm and blues, jazz, and rock. I became intrigued by the rhythm of salsa music. In the Spanish language, salsa means "sauce." Salsa dancing is my favorite type of spice! Todd and I began to take salsa dance lessons and I never wanted to stop. In my opinion, salsa is intriguing, enlightening and powerful way to dance.

Following my final surgery to replace my skull with a titanium plate, I no longer had to wear the helmet. I sure didn't care to wear it ever again. A friend from Spain and his wife invited us and a large group of people over for an outside dinner. The temperature was warm and the weather beautiful. Knowing that I loved salsa music they started playing it to celebrate my survival. I began moving to the beat while sitting in my chair and glory arose from my heart. A small fear arose as I questioned my ability to truly dance as I had prior to the accident. Todd came towards me and reached for my hands to walk with me to the outdoor floor. No one else was dancing. I was stunned that Todd started dancing with me with so many people around us. Despite my dizziness, balance, and memory loss, Todd moved to the beat of the salsa music. I began to dance again! My heart, mind and spirit soared with such love, honor and gratitude to God. I was never going to quit dancing especially when surviving such trauma.

Nine months after my accident, I was asked to dance by a friend, Nora, who organizes a dance fest annually. Nora is from Argentina and grew up in such a beautiful area where the community is very gifted in salsa dancing. Children are taught when they are very young. I saw a three-year-old salsa dance on top of a table, like I've never seen before. Nora asked me to Latin dance. I needed a partner but Todd wasn't comfortable performing. Despite my fear, I asked another man to be my dance partner. Before we performed, Nora asked me to tell the audience a piece of my story. Oh my, I was afraid and somewhat dizzy. I hoped the memory loss would leave me. So I shared my story and performed the meringue, at the Iowa Dance Fest, nine months after the accident! My speech therapists were present and cried as they witnessed my ability to speak loudly without a microphone, effectively vocalize despite aphasia, and perform the meringue successfully. Susie Green, my dear friend, was also present and gasped within her response. She felt I displayed true magic as she witnessed me dance this soon after the accident. Susie also thought that my speech improved more than she ever imagined. My sister-in-law Lori felt that my recovery was a miracle and that I was meant to dance again.

In 2011, an incredible Spanish teacher at North Central Junior High School incorporated salsa dancing education into the curriculum near the end of the semester. Students perform better academically when music is placed into their daily regimen (www.musictherapy.com). The Spanish teacher asked if I would be his dance partner. I remember my son Ryan looking uneasy and concerned about my agreement to do this, perhaps out of embarrassment. I had a fantastic time dancing with the kids. They showed such appreciation for being introduced to salsa. Once again, the power of music and incorporation of dance miraculously showed the simple way to heal, nurture and educate the mind, body and spirit. To this day, I move, sway and smile as I hear the melody, blend, and rhythm of music. This occurs anywhere such as at a movie theater, restaurant, or choir concert. My embarrassed children look in my direction and shake their head "no" to me. Despite their humiliation, I keep on moving to the beat with a grin on my face. A brain injury survivor recently gave me a purple T-shirt which states, "Life is short, dance often."

The Humanities of Writing

In the 1300s, Latin and Greek educators created humanities as a field that studied literature, philosophy, and the arts throughout numerous cultures. I have learned the essence of incorporating the humanities into the education of all health care providers. Therefore, humanities-based communication is the art of all health care. I find it fascinating that a new class, offered by the Stanford School of Medicine, is entitled "The Art and Science of Emotional Intelligence." Prior to my disabilities, I had no clue that this type of a course was available, especially for medical students! Was my memory of proper

medical education completely lost? Last year I went to a conference at the University Of Iowa College Of Medicine. The
title was "Writing, Humanities and the Art of Medicine: Total
Brain Injury and Healing Humanities." My mouth burst open
in utter shock and my brain questioned its true existence.

While I'm currently writing my story, pieces of my memory returned. In 2011, I was contacted by Leslie Finer, from
the Art's Share Program at the University of Iowa. Master's students were creating an anthology of the Patient Voice Project.
This was funded by a grant from Johnson and Johnson/Society
for the Arts in Healthcare and a grant from the Iowa Arts
Council. Additional support was provided by the University
of Iowa's College of Liberal Arts and Sciences. I have no idea
how they knew to contact me, another miracle placed itself
into my life. Leslie asked if I was willing to write my story in
a book they were working on entitled *Progression*. This book
was written by many individuals who shared their health care
adventure. I agreed but knew I needed so much assistance
because of my disabilities. My challenges included difficulty
writing an accurate sentence, poor understanding of the uses
of words, very slow writing or typing, recollection of how to
use a computer, fatigue, and becoming easily overloaded.

Joyce Turner, a graduate student, became my editor.
She willingly came to my house since I was not able to
drive because of my seizures. Based on the grant restric-
tions, Joyce could come one hour, once a week and could
not work with me beyond an eight week time period. My
mind swirled and I questioned my capability to truly master writing my story. My memory was so lost. Joyce was
an amazing editor who reassured and guided me on the
right path. Lo and behold, my story, "Surviving Traumatic
Brain Injury from a Bike Accident," is a chapter in the book
Progression. Recently, I realized the significance of the book's

title. Progression is defined in the dictionary as "a forward movement in time or place which is slow but steady." To me it proves that despite the misery and challenges we experience in life, healing occurs within a progression of events.

When I held the book for the first time and began to slowly read it, I was stunned and bewildered by the reality. Once again I witnessed the power of not only reading my own story but stories of others' life experiences. It was an enriching and compelling avenue to improve my developmental process, create emotional healing, gives me a degree of control, and provides an opportunity to VOICE my life experience.

As I ventured through writing my story, from the past to present day, numerous confusion and shock presented themselves. Sometimes large waves flowed in my direction. It was profound how my memory of the past resurfaced and further improvement swam within my brain's structure and being. My life's purpose began to show itself from birth forward, something I never knew materialized.

CHAPTER 19

The Essence within Disabilities

Annually, 1.4 million in the United States experience a brain injury with 5.3 million living with long-term disabilities (United States Brain Injury Alliance). One out of every four people in our country has disabilities and 70 percent of them are unemployed. I had become another statistic and was angry about it. Accidents, especially severe head injuries, change people without warning. Who was this person looking at me in the mirror? How did the woman whom I was before leave me? Where did I go?

Physicians, such as neuropsychologists and neurologists, informed me numerous times that 90 percent of traumatic brain injury patients lose their previous employment! In such a serious voice with a plank dull look on their face, I was told, "Bridgid, you can't talk effectively with your aphasia to either patients or their families. You have lost your health care knowledge secondary to your memory loss. In addition, you are easily fatigued and have epilepsy!" I did not agree at all. I denied their bogus knowledge base. I find it disheartening when a patient is given such negativity and no further information about resourses for future employment. Please give us hope and simple direction and guidance for what we truly *can* accomplish. Nurses facilitating the continuation of my nursing license stated that I should be labeled 'retired' to stop the cost of continuing to use my license. How dare they say that when I was in my forties, not sixty-five! I needed adequate time to work through my brain's thought processes including anger.

In contrast, other nurses often stated, "You look and sound fine. Come back and work as a volunteer!" My cognitive abilities and speech aphasia had improved somewhat. And I could walk more effectively. But people didn't "get it" that I still had limitations - many that were not visible – and I cried so often trying to explain them. I sobbed at the thought of holding a child who needed emotional support knowing that I was still a mess myself. How would this truly support the child?

Yes, I struggled with anger, major depression, and mental self-punishment. I began to truly understand that I could no longer speak effectively to children and their parents. How could I effectively answer their questions? How would I correctly read, understand, write, or type patient notes appropriately and within a reasonable time frame? What knowledge would I recall and maintain in regards to a patient's health history and current alterations or changes in their present condition? Why on earth did I believe I could work sufficiently eight or twelve hour shifts? Extensive fatigue has never disappeared. After about a five-hour time period, I start to experience poor concentration, confusion, near tears, nausea, dizziness, and the need for silence emerges. My neurological system requires at least a two hour nap daily in a very quiet place. Over time I have learned that when the day has begun with periods of stress, anxiety or sadness, I need even more sleep, often three hours. As I mentioned earlier, insufficient sleep risks the development of seizures.

Why didn't God take me to heaven? What on earth is my purpose in life anymore? Do I have any gifts? Fear pulls us downward into a depth whereby we forget what our life's purpose is. My aunt Katie stated, "Bridgid, God has other plans for you now, a way to share your story and help others. You will always be able to nurture and help others. God's not through with you yet. Your work here isn't finished. You are a walking miracle." No matter what people said, I couldn't hear them. I questioned and doubted my true potential toward the future. Therefore, I had no idea how to truly move forward and away from denial.

CHAPTER 20

What On Earth Is Vocational Rehabilitation?

A wonderful brain injury friend knew I wished to obtain employment as a health care provider. He encouraged me to contact Vocational Rehabilitation. I questioned what on earth he was talking about! I assume my lack of knowledge regarding the name and meaning of Voc Rehab was due to my memory loss or that I was never told of this prior to my accident. Vocational rehabilitation is "a process which enables persons with functional, psychological, developmental, cognitive and emotional impairments or health conditions to overcome barriers to accessing, maintaining or returning to employment or other useful occupation" (wikipedia.org). My friend explained this more clearly and simply to me. Voc Rehab would help me obtain a part-time job, suitable for me. What employment position would I perceive as appropriate, based on my experience as a nurse practitioner that would enhance my self-esteem and self-worth? Many times, I frequently questioned, was I truly disabled enough to obtain this assistance? What right did I have to apply for vocational rehabilitation when so many have more disabilities than I do!

Despite my fear, self-confidence erupted in my spirit, and I followed his suggestions and applied. Shockingly, each disability of mine is listed on Voc Rehab's criteria for services. In Iowa, you generally wait a year for the state to determine your disability. I slowly relearned how to type and utilize a computer to establish the data required for placement. I needed so much help completing the confusing and overwhelming paperwork. Remarkably, nine months after I applied, Vocational Rehabilitation was initiated.

I wanted to put my fear behind me, move out of confusion and denial and get on with my life. To begin this process, I slowly read what Todd and Mom wrote on www.carepages. com. The number of people who were on this website was incredible. Exchanging information regarding my status in this way rather than having to respond to numerous overwhelming phone calls was so valuable for my family. Todd and my mom updated my status on a daily basis and always asked for so many prayers for healing. So many prayers were provided to us, and Mom states that one thousand or more people were aware of my accident, as I was also listed on a national prayer chain. When I began to review the daily aspects of my hospitalizations I was scared and denied this patient was truly me.

With much assistance, I then began to read my hospital records which took awhile and brought so many tears. Once again much relearning of my previous medical knowledge base required much research on my part and input from many health care professionals. I continued to remain in utter shock and questioned so many times that health care professionals really couldn't truly be writing about me! I then began to compare the events that occurred between my care page and medical records to visualize the situations occurring on the similar dates of time. The information I received was an incredible process for my brain to comprehend, adjust to and begin to understand.

Since it was still very difficult to utilize a computer, Todd got me a voice recorder where I voiced those sentences that I felt were significant enough to capture information from both the hospital records and care page notes. Tears flowed down my face not only from reading what occurred but the loss of my ability to write, interpret simple information, poor concentration, confusion, organization, and frustration. Therefore, my disabilities circled through continued outrage and depression. I repeatedly felt as I was not who I was before.

Despite my life's turmoil, a flame within my soul erupted as I swam through such a challenging tide. I continued to swim within my brain's whirlwind waves, grasping for healing that can arise from suffering. I was never going to quit. Yes, I am a mover and shaker. In essence, I wanted to somehow share my life's dilemma with everyone! My sister-in-law Lori shared with me the name of a man whom she contacted when I was in a coma. Patrick Sterenchuk is a spiritual and intuitive counselor who helps others to heal. He told Lori that the angels were determining if I would live or die. If I lived, I would start sharing my personal survival story to others!

Besides my medical written records, I obtained my CTs and MRI. I have a friend, a radiologist who came to my home to view my CTs and MRI with Todd and me. His eyes opened widely as if in shock from what he saw. At one point in time he shook his head with a blank look on his face and wouldn't say why. He helped incredibly to place the CTs and MRI pictures onto Microsoft PowerPoint slides. My husband, that amazing electrical engineer, also placed pictures on further slides of me while in a coma, after a seizure and when I was finally returned home.

I then began to research the overall impacts surrounding traumatic brain injury including physiological, cognitive, mental health, and family dynamics. My intent was to learn the essential needs required to heal one's mind, body, and spirit. I was blown away when I discovered so many similarities between other brain injury survivors in their own journey. Serendipity emerged when a brain injury survivor's experience linked within mine. I was not alone. Once you begin to understand your disabilities, especially when they correspond to others, you become real again.

This provided incredible validation of this lifelong disease. I dove within my brain's whirlwind grasping ways to create a vessel to display healing that can arise from suffering. Miracles continued to enter my life. Slowly, I structured a PowerPoint presentation from the beginning of my accident on through the up-and-down aspects of my recovery. A mystical feeling soared within me. I wanted to somehow help educate health care professionals and provide hope to survivors and their advocates. I strived to share and support healing which can arise in defiance of the challenges that emerge from brain injury.

As I reflect back in time, my brain recalls that I was in an elective speech class at Wahlert, a large Catholic high school. I was self-conscious and had a great fear of public speaking. So I wanted to run away from this class. But we were required to speak publicly to classmates. Despite my fear, I proceeded. Following my first public speaking experience, my teacher personally shared that I was a great public speaker! I was in shock and didn't understand why he even said this! This would become a tool of my future—something I was incapable of seeing at that time.

In the fall of 2009, one and a half years after my accident, I shared my documented survival story for the first time. Although it is still hard for me to believe, I spoke to faculty and speech therapy students at Wendell Johnson, the University of Iowa Speech and Hearing Center. These wonderful people were continuing to help me with my aphasia. Within a classroom, I placed a PowerPoint presentation with slides onto a screen for the audience to witness. I'm sure Todd and faculty helped me get this all processed. I asked angels to guide and assist me in my ability to speak. Lo and behold, I was able to present my story vocally for one hour, despite my aphasia. Speech therapists intuitively knew the words that I was trying to verbalize since they understood my aphasia whereas the general public may not have.

One student whom I had always adored working with began crying and cried to the extent that she had a hard time stopping and left the room for a moment. Another student was tearful as well and their instructor's mouths opened in utter amazement. I was told so many different times, "Bridgid, we have never seen anyone with traumatic brain injury and aphasia improve to the enormous degree that you have!" Unfortunately, I didn't interpret nor understand what on earth they were saying. It is only recently that I have begun to understand all the divine messages sent for me to truly understand. They were describing and embracing all the miracles that came my way. My mind, body and spirit continued to readjust further, as I proceeded to excel in my endeavors. Quitting was not an option in my spirit. I felt a need to further succeed in presenting the dynamics of my story. My ability to read improved further when I was able to explore my medical records in more depth. The reality of what truly happened during my hospitalizations erupted. I questioned and denied these tragedies. With much determination I chose to move forward, out and away from tragedy toward where my heart and spirit guided me to heal. I created a large part of my healing journey through restoring and re-defining myself. Despite my obstacles, a dream arose. Reconnecting to health care in some way, shape or form was my mission. I visualized ways to share the tragic aspects of my brain injury and the dynamics of my healing process.

In November 2009, one year and five months since my accident, colleagues asked me to share my story at Nursing Grand Rounds at the University of Iowa Hospital and Clinics. Many of my colleagues were present as well as my occupational therapist and rehabilitation physician. Despite the residual symptoms from my stroke of numbness, tingling and weakness in my left leg, I was able to walk to that podium with success. The smiles that arose from my colleagues brought me such joy. I was at least professionally present with them in an educational setting. Who of those present didn't believe that I would maintain true survival? Who believed in miracles? Did my presentation impact the audience in any way?

One of my colleagues, Susie Green, heard me present my story. Susie shared, "You, like always, know your audience and how to get your message across. That is how you were as a nurse practitioner too. You know how to just be YOU! My reassurance came from that realization that despite the damage that your brain had endured, YOU were YOU!"

In the fall of 2009, my sister-in-law Karin was taking a web design class. One of the projects for the students was to create and design a website of their choice. Karin knew I had shared my brain injury story a couple of times at hospitals but was well aware of my desire to somehow verge my pathway further forward. She felt my story touched everyone who heard me present. Karin knew that I was driven to educating others by illustrating the trauma I experienced with brain injury and the variety of treatments I explored for further healing to emerge. Karin believed that to create a website would get such dynamic information out to the public. I was so honored when Karin asked me if she could create a website to further educate others. My dream was to become a motivational speaker. I agreed to her fabulous idea and was so honored and extremely grateful for the divine offering she sent my way. She utilized a software program entitled Dreamweaver. When Karin shared the name of this software my eyes opened widely as the words dream and weaver are very powerfully combined together. Dream is defined as an "aspiration, a goal or aim." Whereas the definition of weaver states "a form by combining various elements or details into a connected whole." Karin illustrated one of her incredible gifts being a website artist and marketer. Naturally, Karin received an A in her web design class! Another miraculous dream fired into another one of my pathways.

I am not cognizant of how my mission traveled to other cities in Iowa. For whatever reason, I was asked to present my journey at the Iowa Brain Injury Alliance Conference in Des Moines, Iowa, March 2010. From this venture, Dubuque Iowa, asked me to present at Finley Hospital in March as well. I had the opportunity to meet Patrick Sterenchuk. Patrick is the spiritual healer whom Lori had spoken to when I was hospitalized. When Lori introduced me and said my first name, Patrick's eyes opened wide. He smiled so brightly and walked toward me and gently placed his arms around me in a hug, stating, "You're truly here on this earth!"

I presented my story the next day at Finley Hospital. Unbelievably, Patrick introduced me and shared with others the miracle of my survival and his excitement that I was alive and present in that very room. My step uncle video-taped my presentation and later I was shown the video. Tears rolled down my face and numbness surrounded me, as this truly didn't happen to me! Denial continued to plummet back and forth. The best part of my presentation focused on honoring my dear mother for all the tremendous heal-ing gifts she gave me and our family. So many feel that I am the real me now but sometimes my understanding of my impact towards others was hard for me to absorb. I was dazed and didn't believe as if I was stranded in a cloud.

I am often very hard on myself. Memories of working directly as a nurse practitioner in a hospital setting and my inability to no longer do that still brought such sadness. All these years' people have voiced, "Bridgid, although you can't clinically practice as a pediatric nurse practitioner again, you are still a nurse." I often cried, as I questioned whether being an educated health care professional even existed. I couldn't afford to maintain the cost of license renewal nor the necessary continuing education. I still felt as if I was a failure as the time, education and commitment I had to my position appeared lost. Rumination, or the tendency to get stuck and dwell on failures, is often a consequence of traumatic brain injury.

In sadness, confusion, and grief, I decided to con-tact Patrick Sterenchuk. He was such a divine person for me to connect with. I was driving when I parked my car along the Iowa River. I felt snuggled in the beautiful bright sky with the river so near to me. In our conversation, Patrick tried to encourage me to press forward. He dis-played such a tender belief in my further abilities. Patrick stated, "Bridgid you are helping people heal in so many ways. You are going to continue sharing your story multi-ple times to the point that you will be on television." Before ending our conversation, Patrick called me his "sister." I questioned if precious Patrick was truly losing his mind.

As I drove home, I went over a bridge above the Iowa River. Not too far from the right side of the bridge on the shore twenty to thirty bald eagles showed me their presence! I have never seen so many bald eagles located so close together, ever! My mouth gasped open and tears rolled down my face. Unfortunately, I couldn't stop the car right there or I'd stop all traffic. There was no way for me to visualize them even closer. The beautiful bald eagle, the national emblem of the United States, is embraced as a spirit guide and a chief over all feathered animals. I have learned that the presence of a bald eagle represents life that is reborn.

Native Americans believe that an eagle encourages you to move upward in your journey and believe in your ability to further succeed beyond your previous self vision. Courage within you will emerge despite a challenging time whereby your strength and endurance will enhance and a new life beginning will unfold. Therefore, this is a spiritual awakening and a larger opportunity for a further relationship to the Divine. I was bewildered about my future, not visualizing what Patrick remarked, that truly could ever occur. Again, I continued to receive so many messages of my near future.

CHAPTER 21

Earth Angels

I began taking physiology in high school, which I enjoyed. But I often compared myself to other students. Was I as smart as the other students? Sister Ginnie, a precious nun, was an amazing physiology teacher who inspired confidence in me. Toward the end of the semester we had to dissect infant pigs. Ginnie asked me to insert a needle of formaldehyde into the pigs before dissection. I was shocked that she asked me and somewhat frightened. But I did it. She believed in me from the very start. My dream of caring for others was vague, but the potential was inspired through Ginnie. Many years later after my injury, Ginnie returned to be a part of my life. Her presence was delightful. She demonstrated such optimism in my health care journey. Her guidance and reconnection validated what would become my new life's purpose.

Ginnie has been a dear family friend for so very long. She completed the doctorate in Family Counseling in the College of Education and Curriculum Coordinator at the University Of Iowa College Of Medicine. She saw me daily when I was hospitalized, praying for my recovery. Ginnie always knew when I was in pain which she visualized and thus sensed.

When my life began to blossom, Ginnie was hospitalized for cancer. I went to visit her during her own suffering. In her physiological discomfort, Ginnie stated that I will present my story to medical students. Ginnie is the first person to show me her belief in my ability to now speak to medical students. I denied the possibility because I did not feel that I was capable. My mouth hung open and tears fell from my eyes. Believe it or not, I did present to over two hundred medical students and their staff at the University of Iowa in May of 2010. I thank God that I've received Ginnie's confidence numerous times in my life. Unfortunately, Ginnie died of gallbladder cancer, but in her pathway to death she continued to serve others. Her death brought me such sorrow. She believed, healed and supported me and so many people. I will always be so very grateful for all Ginnie ministered to me.

When my children were in elementary school, Jane, a fantastic school counselor, visited me while I was in a coma. Jane asked Todd if a friend of hers, Mary Thompson, could come visit me. Mary Thompson, MA, is a holistic practitioner, Reiki master and spiritual minister of healing touch. During this time, Todd feared my prognosis as he witnessed me lying in a coma. Therefore, he was so willing to have anyone provide me with alternative care as he knew well that I always valued its importance. I have no memory of Mary providing me Reiki when I was hospitalized.

Mary has maintained her powerful presence in my life. She came to my home to visit as well as provide me Reiki, such gentle profound healing. Ryan and Molly witnessed Reiki provided to me. They learned some of the basic skills of Reiki. Mary became such a dear friend. Prior to Mary practicing Reiki, she suffered from a brain tumor. Such a blessed opportunity to contact with another brain injured survivor. Physicians were unable to biopsy Mary's deep growth or provide any treatment. Facing the fearful outcome for more than a year, Mary learned the importance of complementary healing. Finally, after a risky surgery, miracles presented themselves and a healthy Mary was here to stay!

Prior to her brain tumor, Mary worked as a speech therapist at Madonna Brain Injury Rehabilitation Hospital in Lincoln, Nebraska. Madonna is one of the top ten rehabilitation hospitals in the United States which serves traumatic brain injury, spinal cord injury, stroke and pulmonary condition. In the 1640s, the name Madonna provided the dignity of the Blessed Virgin Mary. Madonna is viewed as a religious figure in both Christianity and Islam. She is recognized as a spiritual mother, the queen of the angels, and a woman who provides all with divine grace.

My friend Mary was skilled in so many entities. She completely understood my aphasia and how appropriately to speak with me. One day a colleague of Mary's who worked at Madonna wanted to visit with me. After we finished conversing, she unbelievably asked if I would consider speaking to faculty and brain injury survivors at Madonna! I was in shock. She didn't even know me and spoke to me for such a short time. Naturally though in complete honor, I said "yes" to present at Madonna.

In July 2010, Mary traveled with me on the trip to Lincoln, Nebraska. Mary was the only one who could drive since I had lost that privilege to drive secondary to seizures. Mary shared so much about her experience at Madonna as a speech therapist. The closer we came to Nebraska, my heart and emotions were triggered. I thought about the pediatric patients at Madonna and my prior experience working to help children heal. Tears emerged as I reentered my grief recalling the loss of my role as a pediatric nurse practitioner.

I was honored to view Madonna's incredible rehabilitation hospital and apartments for outpatients and families. In addition, they have a large building designed for cardiac and weight lifting exercise area, a pool, massage therapists, chiropractic care, meditation, and a labyrinth to walk around outside. The labyrinth is a spiritual movement on a circular trail that has been used for over four thousand years by many cultures and religions. This was designed to give our brains clarity, insight, and calmness though our life's transformation. My brain was in shock and utter amazement regarding all the incredible health care services Madonna provides. I had never seen a hospital that administers such vast healing opportunities.

Daily they communicate as a team on a patient's behalf. A team approach is a necessary entitlement for a patient to receive from health care professionals. As opposed to having only one health care professional's opinion of where the patient's life is headed. The transferred negativity of a patient's outcome initiates fear, depression, and potential loss of purpose. Learning the tremendous value of a team approach instantaneously took me back in time when I was in rehabilitation. This provided another learning opportunity of the best ways to be treated as a recovering brain injury survivor. Give us HOPE!

A huge message that I received was their dynamic principle that a health care provider never makes expectations or decisions on their own, in all aspects of a patient's recovery. Team approach produces excellence in recovery. Growth in rehabilitation is a very slow process. Health care professionals and family need to honor every tiny improvement made by patients in rehabilitation. Madonna inspires patients on a daily basis to work toward a small simple goal for the day. Staff honor and support their process no matter how tiny the improvement is. Daily affirmation is essential.

CHAPTER 22

Divine Messages from Children

The CEO of Madonna, Martha Lommel, MA, MBA, FACHE, was aware that I was a pediatric nurse practitioner. Thus she wanted me to initially visit the pediatric rehabilitation area of the hospital. My stomach twirled with fear of the potential trauma that I may witness. Could I proceed forward witnessing the health care I missed? As they opened the door, a four year old boy raced toward the door with such excitement and enthusiasm displayed on his face. As he ran toward me, he smiled at me with such a grin on his cheeks. I naturally smiled right back at him and waived hello. He then walked towards me reaching for my hand. He gently grasped my hand, held on to it, and kissed it! I was stunned, that he approached me in this manner—especially since he did not know me at all. I was a stranger to him! As I walked past him my tears gently fell from my eyes and this experience tremendously impacted me.

In astonishment, I learned that he suffered from the similar origin of brain trauma that I did and was going to be discharged that day. He mistakenly ventured on a small scooter down the driveway to the street below and unfortunately was hit by a car. I walked away with my heart so open as well as my brain questioning, did this experience really occur? Today I finally understand that he was sending me a message which I desperately needed to see, feel and believe. I needing the insight he provided me that my role as a pediatric nurse practitioner didn't disappear with my disabilities. The Divine was reminding me that I will always maintain my connection with children whether I'm in direct practice as a nurse practitioner or not.

I remember today that children at young ages are so very connected to the Divine, as if they are divine messengers. They have a deep relationship with a higher power which we as aging adults generally lose or diminish in some way, shape or form. Children remind us of the blessings for which we should be grateful. They provide us with purposeful information about today and the future. They energize the value and principles of spirituality. This precious young boy showed me that, despite my disabilities, I continued to exhibit connection to children. He also enthusiastically demonstrated the true feeling of such joy, enthusiasm and determination of walking through the recovery process.

Toward the end of the day, a three-year-old girl was successfully walking with her mother. Sadly, at nine months of age, she suffered traumatic brain injury secondary to significant mistreatment by a child care provider. She had to relearn every aspect from birth to her current age of three. This included vision, ambulation, cognition, speech, you name it. Once again, health care providers were amazed by her miraculous survival which was well beyond their level of understanding.

On that particular day, she was walking with her mother through various areas of the hospital. When she walked closer to people she portrayed such an incredibly beautiful smile. She placed her hands together as if she was to pray and then opened her praying hands and moved her arms toward you. Initially she did not share anything verbally until her mother said, "Tell them what you feel." She looked back at her mother and then returned her presence to the person in front of her and stated, "I'm sending you the angels." This young girl was very well aware of the power of the angels and their presence with her. She sent a profound message for us to hear. Those amazing angels were always present with us.

In my mind, children are and always will be healers and messengers from the Divine. In my research I have uncovered that many people feel that children are clairvoyant and on a journey down from the spirit and thus a holy child of God. In the book entitled *Black Elk Speak,* Black Elk, an Oglala Lakota holy man, shares, "Grown men may learn from very little children for the hearts of little children are pure, and, therefore, the Great Spirit may show to them many things that older people miss." A child is seen as a symbol towards the very act of healing. During the ages of birth to seven years of age, Thomas Armstrong reports, *In the Radiant Child*, that children are channels of healing which is shared through their unconscious.

Recently, I had a recollection of a children's book that I wrote in graduate school entitled *I Grow as You Grow.* The symbolism of this book illustrates a grandfather's willingness to take in the messages that children deliver and produce insight to us as they are growing in development. The story depicts the struggles an eight year old boy is experiencing.

He so wanted to be older so that he would fit in more with older children. He sensed that no one really heard nor responded to his needs. The boy's grandfather guides him through the emotional and cognitive development stage of the child's life from birth to eight years of age and demonstrates not only what the child learned at each stage but more importantly, what the grandfather learned from the child.

The boy I met at Madonna Hospital was four years of age. When a child is four, empathy begins to arise in his development. He understands when a person is feeling sad or hurt. In my mind's eye, he sensed my emotions. Therefore, he may visualize the essence of giving someone a hug or a kiss when someone is hurting. In such gratitude of today's understanding, I received such an angelic gift from him. As I reread the book *I Grow as You Grow* today, I understand the profound messages angels sent from the two precious children I encountered at Madonna Hospital. They appeared to sense that I was grieving. Any of us have the capability to embrace the insight and healing that children send us. Children also need the emotional support that we do. Adults can learn and relearn so very much growth from children if we just take the time to observe and listen to their profound messages. Following my presentation to the health care staff, I was in utter shock and gratitude, though I knew it wasn't possible, when Martha asked me to work as a pediatric nurse practitioner at Madonna! Following in September, I presented to Adult and Child Neurosurgical conference and in October a pediatric nursing conference. These precious children paved my way. Unbelievably, after the adult and child neurological conference a woman whom I didn't know came up to me afterward. Andee was holding me and crying so very much. She had the willingness to share that she was a nurse who took care of me in both the ICU and step-down unit who didn't believe that I would ever survive! It was a privilege for me to meet her and show miracles in action.

One summer after my accident, my family vacationed in beautiful Jackson Hole, Wyoming to visit my brother Peter, his wife Mimi, and their son William. Being in the presence of the mountains is so moving and very nurturing to my spirit. Sitting outside of their home is mesmerizing as they live in an incredibly dynamic place where mountains circle around you. One day I asked four-year-old William if he'd like me to read him a children's book. He stated sure and handed me one of his favorites—a book designed to share information about firefighters. I began reading the words slowly, as that is my process in reading effectively. A couple of times William would remark, "No, Bridgid, it's like this," referring to the sentence that I read inaccurately. William had this book read to him often and therefore he understood exactly how to precisely reread the sentence to me. At first, my heart rate raced and my brain felt such dilemma. I thought my tears would fall, as my four year old nephew was re-teaching me how to read appropriately. Surprisingly, I interchanged my deteriorating self-esteem to move toward gratitude. William was graciously guiding me. At four years of age, he seemed to understand my disability. He verbalized without negative facial expressions that I was not stupid. Again, even though he was a child, he must have known I was hurting. He taught me gently in a kind manner the mistakes I had made. This is symbolic of my need to continue re-learning daily and see the areas I still need improvement on, without shame. He smiled at the end of the story and picked another book.

William and I went for a walk on a glorious mountain trail. He often ran a bit ahead of me showing his pride beating me, which was adorable. On the way back down the trail, William was walking much slower and shared that he was tired. William looked whipped and made me aware that he might not make it the rest of the way. But he didn't want to quit. He gently placed his arms all the way around my upper leg and held us close together. The look on his face made me smile. He showed such relief as his arms held onto my legs, side by side. William appeared uplifted and began to share such wonderful things with me. This in and of itself was a delightful experience. I had not seen William for over a year when he was three. We were at a family reunion with so many people, and thus I hardly had the chance to truly meet him. William also trusted me to help him move forward, despite us hardly knowing each other very well. Children were giving me messages that I had a hard time accepting. Yes, I witnessed the divine connection I still have to children. This has been delivered through a child despite the alterations in my life that have taken me away from working with them directly as a pediatric nurse practitioner.

CHAPTER 23

Television, Radio, and Publications

In January of 2010, Joyce Turner, the editor helping me write a chapter in the book *Progression: An Anthology of the Patient Voice Project,* utterly surprised me. Joyce asked if I would speak with her on the Iowa Public Radio Talk Program entitled *The Exchange.* I agreed since we were going to provide this together about the beauty of writing. I was scared as I was unaware of questions I would be asked. Joyce discussed the implications of the power of healing when you write your personal story. A woman who works with those disabled from the military spoke as well. She encourages her patients to write their personal story. Unfortunately, many felt they couldn't as they were informed to never share their true experience. This infuriated me and many others as well. I shared a short section of a paragraph that I'd written in the book. My aphasia kicked in probably more from my fear and brought me to tears of embarrassment. Joyce helped me communicate what I was trying to say.

Unbelievably, from this time forward, I was asked to share my story on Public Access Television in December 2010. Their focus was on educating the public regarding reasons, impacts and successes of those disabled. In January 2011, the chapter that I wrote entitled "Surviving Traumatic From a Bicycle Accident" was placed as a blog provided by Lash and Associates Publishing (www.lapublishing.com), the only publishers in the United States which provide incredible literature for everyone impacted by brain injury, even health care providers!

When Vocational Rehabilitation is working with those starting a small business they provide technical and financial assistance. Vocational Rehab recommended Christoph Truemper, a website and graphic designer, in April 2011 to further embellish my website www.bridgidruden.com. He taught me how to update the website and alter or change any mistakes that I made, which were frequent. I was placed on Facebook along with designs of my logo, business cards, flyer, banner, thank you cards, letterhead and poster. In the spring of 2014, Christoph helped me create a poster presentation articulating my story. I can't even begin to thank Christoph for all the work he has done to enhance my journey of establishing a small business, something I never thought, felt, or saw for my future. Christoph has been such a pleasure to worth with and has blown me away with all of the talents he has.

In July 2011, the book *Progression: an Anthology of the Patient Voice Project* was published. I'm still bewildered by how on earth this occurred, obviously not on my own but through the grace of God. My life's excursion continued to blossom. In November of 2013, I was interviewed by Janie Smith, the founder of the *Hope Beyond Trauma* radio show. Janie Smith is the author of *Hope Beyond Trauma…a Mother's Journey*. She communicates with passion from her own challenges her family experienced during their anguish. She guides people to move from trauma, to HOPE, triumph, and inspiration! This was a privilege for me to visit with both Janie Smith and John Hatten, a rehabilitation counselor, who is a traumatic brain injury survivor, on their radio show. Janie shared, "I really enjoyed meeting and interviewing you. Your candor, courage and determination is amazing and an inspiration to all of us!"

CHAPTER 24

My Gifted Mother

Mom has thirty years of nursing experience and is certified as an occupational health nurse and case manager. She was skilled in so many areas including advocating for those injured. This time in her life she advocated for me. My mom is a compelling and loving mother who never left my bedside. She wrote a daily journal signifying the up-and-down days of the healing process. Mom entitled this compelling journal, "The Rebirth of Bridgid." She describes the pain she experienced watching me learn to walk, read, write and communicate again, as if I was three years old, and the tremendous impact this had on our family. During painful times Mom would reflect on the word "Pause," with the following acronyms: P, peaceful; A, answer; U, under; S, stressful; E, event. At that time she would practice breathing slowly inward with courage filling her soul and then fear was to escape as she breathed outward.

The most heartwarming and powerful part of my journey occurred when my mother was asked to share her experience as a mother of a brain injury survivor. In March 2012, Mom presented at the Iowa Brain Injury Association annual conference, entitled Family and Advocates: Navigating Brain Injury. Mom and Todd creatively constructed a dynamic PowerPoint presentation illustrating her struggle during such hardship. Mom's presentation is extremely moving, touching and sends profound messages to all. The magnificent title of Mom's presentation is "Trust the Process: From Compost...to True Life." My mother shares:

"This symbolized for us how all of our life experiences are like compost...fertile ground for new growth. Recovery from brain injury is a lifelong healing process for the survivor and their family. There will be bumps in the road and challenges to face in the days ahead. The recovery process is one of holding on and letting go, accepting the 'new normal,' sometimes taking two steps forward and one back, and living one day at a time with hope and courage. Our transformation to this new way of living, as with compost, takes time. This process requires patience and acceptance which places courage, faith and trust to the test. Our Higher Power can make something good out of what is difficult in our lives. This transformation will take time, patience, and trust in that Higher Power. Before we can truly help and support our family members we must begin this amazing process through taking excellent care of ourselves first. We, too, need transformation from discouragement, anger, resentment, and hopelessness. The recovery process is fertile ground for this transformation through family, faith, friends and a Higher Power. We need willingness to act our way into good living in our new life for transformation to take place. Then we will experience despair and

hopelessness turned to hope, loneliness to friendships, isolation to openness, close mindedness to willingness, critical thinking to compassion, fear to faith and illness to recovery. Trust the process and wait for the sweet surprises of our Higher Power."
—Mary Jeananne Fremann

At the end of Mom's presentation, she encourages everyone to hold hands as if you're holding the hands of your best friend or family member. She states, "If we take good care of ourselves only then can we be of true service to others." The picture below is the picture of Molly, Mom, and I holding our hands together with the words: "Live well, Laugh often, and Love much."

CHAPTER 25

Discovering My New Life's Purpose

Bridgid Ruden is a remarkable individual who has faced adversity with a fierce will to move on that will inspire us all to be the best that we can be.

The neurosurgical management of head injury continues to evolve, yet the ability to predict outcome remains an almost random event.

I have no doubt that Bridgid Ruden benefited from being close to a Level I Trauma Center familiar with the care of severe head injury. I know she thanks me for the outcome she has achieved, but the entire team at the University of Iowa Hospitals and Clinics deserves the credit.

The many individuals who have struggled with severe head injury deserve recognition.

It is in support of these severely impacted
patients and families that Bridgid Ruden's
remarkable story needs to be shared.
    She will tell you that it has not been easy.
    She will tell you that life is not what it was.
    She will also tell all of us to not give up hope.
    She will tell you to take each day as it comes, striving
    to bring out the best in yourself
    and in those you love.

—*Timothy Ryken, MD, Neurosurgeon*

When I'm introduced before I present my story, I'm utterly stunned as they share pieces of my bio. At times, I have looked around me and question, "Who is she?" "Where did she come from?" "I'd like to meet her." Before I present to an audience, fear has a tendency to slide its way into me. I have learned the divine power of asking angels to guide me through my voice so that I share what is most beneficial to the audience. My anxiety and fear vanish and I trust in this process. Giving presentations effectively can transmit healing vitality, light, and love. Doreen Virtue notes that Archangel Raphael advised her before she presented. "Don't worry about impressing the audience. Instead, put your whole focus upon blessing them." At the end of my presentation, I share a song entitled "Serenity" and encourage meditation to promote a state of calmness and peace of mind. I finalize with the words, "I honor the spirit that is within you and it is also the spirit within me."

A patient's story guides health care providers to reexamine their medical practice, guides them in developing additional ways toward true healing, and enhances the effectiveness of their treatment. I encourage all to treat others the way they would want to be treated. Health care providers describe my presentation as eye-opening, essential and a marvelous testimony of healing. Those in attendance at my presentation express feeling insightful, personally moved, uplifted and leave with courage and hope which is then incorporated into their own life's journey. Although I assumed my life's mission melted away from my previous persona, I now realize that it never left me. My nursing care has been altered but not denied in its present existence. I now understand the epiphany of my life's venture.

Life is "a corresponding state, existence, or principle of existence conceived of as belonging to the soul." A purpose is "a fixed design, outcome, or idea that is the object of an action or other effort." Disabilities didn't take away my life's purpose. I needed to stop being a victim, release my denial and remove myself away from misery. Therefore, I needed to believe in myself, trust, and truly visualize all the validation, support, and amazing opportunities I've received from God, angels, and so many others. I still have a purpose in this life!

CHAPTER 26

We've Learned and We've Grown

Erma Bombeck states, "There is a thin line that separates laughter and pain, comedy and tragedy, humor and hurt." Despite suffering from a hurricane of brain-altering occurrences, our family was placed into an altered pathway of life. Although I assumed so, God never did forget us. We were given an incredible journey. Our family was pulled in numerous directions, but over time we honor our abilities and learn to adapt successfully. Despite the family's turmoil and suffering, learning from this painful experience is truly enriching and valuable. Pain provides opportunities for growth. Hope and belief in the unknown has been ministered to us. Compassionate love and prayers to one another know no boundaries! We truly believe in the true existence of miracles. Life is so precious and our gratitude is huge. We've learned that life is so short and thus we respect and honor God's purpose for each day, even though it may appear so tiny. Our journey has provided an understanding of the aspects of suffering and thus we've learned how to valuably share so many blessings with others. We as a family are much stronger than we ever knew was possible. Despite the aspects of my disabilities, I have learned and achieved an experience that has returned JOY to my soul. I send you so many blessings and joy to your beautiful mind, body, and spirit.

ACKNOWLEDGEMENTS

- Dr. Yang Ahn
- Erma Bombeck
- Dr. Jane F. Bourgeois
- Angie Cookman
- Kathleen Elletson
- Leslie Finer
- Andrew Freymann
- Brian Freymann
- Don Freymann
- Glen Freymann
- Jeananne Freymann
- Karin Freymann
- Michael Freymann
- Peter Freymann
- William Freymann
- Susie Green
- Jenny Hemesath
- Katie Hemesath
- Kimberly Hemesath
- Lori Hemesath
- Dr. John Hughlings Jackson
- Dr. Robert Jones

- Sherrilyn Kenyon
- Ana King
- Rachel Lauer
- Dr. Andrew Lee
- Mike Lewis
- Katie Miller
- Laura Mullen
- Husam Qadoura
- Meghan Ruden
- Molly Ruden
- Norene Ruden
- Richard Ruden
- Ryan Ruden
- Todd Ruden
- Dr. Tim Ryken
- Dr. Oliver Sack
- Barbara Schreiber
- Joseph Sherlock
- Andee Steciw, RN
- Patrick Sterenchuk
- Greg Thompson
- Mary Thompson
- Tammie Tomash
- Christoph Truember
- Joyce Ellen Turner
- Dr. Carl Young

BIBLIOGRAPHY

"About Epilepsy." *Epilepsy Foundation of North/Central Illinois, Iowa, Nebraska.* Accessed 2015. http://www.epilepsyheartland.org/AboutEpilepsy.

"About Us." *Under Musical Construction.* 2016. http://musictherapy.com/the-right-stuff/.

Armstrong, Thomas. *The Radiant Child.* Wheaton: Guest Books, 1985.

"The Artisan's Stories." *bTizzy.* 2016. http://www.btizzy.com/collections/bposh-artisans.

Blume, Judy. *Are You There God? It's Me, Margaret.* New York: Yearling, 1970.

"Brain Injury Resources." *Lash and Associates Publishing/ Training.* 2009. http://www. lapublishing.com/ blog/tbi-information-resources/abi-brain-injury/ information-acquire-brain-injury/.

"Bridgit." *Baby Names*. Accessed 2015. http://
www.babynames.com/name/Bridgit.

Crigler, Jason. "Defying the Odds: Reclaiming Life."
Presentation at the Brain Injury Affiliation of Iowa
Conference, West Des Moines, IA, March 5, 2015.

Crigler, Jason, and Marie Crigler. *Defying the Odds,
Reclaiming Life*. YouTube video. 17:21. February
22, 2013. http://youtu.be/YzWE6ArfquE.

Darling, David. Serenity. Cella Blue CD.2001

Dwelle, Jessica, and Leslie Finer, eds. *Progression:
An Anthology of the Patient Voice Project*.
Iowa City: Patient Voice Project, 2011.

Farmer, Steven. *Animal Spirit Guide*. New
York: Hay House, 2006.

"Founder's Story: Janet Mentgen and the Healing Touch
Story." *Healing Touch Program*. 2015. http://www.
healingtouchprogram.com/about/founder-s-story.

Kreutzer, Jeffrey, and Lauren Taylor. *Getting Better
and Better After Brain Injury: A Guide for
Families, Friends and Caregivers*. Richmond:
Virginia Commonwealth University, 1999.

Lecture from "PSYCH 1345: The Art and Science of
Emotional Intelligence." at Stanford School of Medicine,
Stanford, NJ, 2015. http://explorecourses.stanford.edu.

McLachlan, Sarah. "I Will Remember You." YouTube video, 3:39. November 3, 2006. https://www.youtube.com/watch?v=nSz16ngdsG0.

Muller, Romeo, and Robert May. "Misfits" in *Rudolph the Red Nosed Reindeer*, YouTube video, 1:17:14. November 19, 2012. https://www.youtube.com/watch?v=RwY6ZNmV1OU.

"Music Therapy in Response to Crisis and Trauma." *American Music Therapy Association.* Accessed 2015. http://www.musictherapy.org/assets/1/7/MT_Crisis_2006.pdf.

Neihardt, John G. *Black Elk Speaks.* New York: William Morrow & Company, 1932.

Olcott, Chauncey, and George Graff. "When Irish Eyes Are Smiling." YouTube video, 3:36. October 19, 2011. https://www.youtube.com/watch?v=KHSV8igDiEo.

Osborn, Claudia. *Over My Head: A Doctor's Own Story of Head Injury from the Inside Looking Out.* Kansas City: Andrews McMeel, 2000.

"Our Mission." *Brain Injury Alliance of Iowa.* Accessed 2016. www.biaia.org.

"Reiki history in change." *Reiki.nu.* 2009. http://www.reiki.nu/history.html.

"Resources." *Epilepsy Foundation of North/Central Illinois, Iowa, Nebraska.* Accessed 2015. http://www.epilepsyheartland.org/Resources.

Ruden, Bridgid. "Surviving Traumatic Brain Injury from a Bike Accident," in *Progression: An Anthology of the Patient Voice Project*, edited by Jessica and Leslie Finer, 134–140. Iowa City: Patient Voice Project, 2011.

Ruden, Bridgid. "Bereavement Follow-Up: An Opportunity to Extend Nursing Care." *The Journal of Pediatric Oncology Nursing* 13, no. 4 (1995): 219–225, doi: 10.1177/104345429601300407.

Shields, David and Thomas Brown. "Family Support Re-defined." Presented at Community Neurorehab, Iowa City, IA. March 5, 2015.

Smith, Janie. *Hope Beyond Trauma . . . a Mother's Journey.* Campbell: Fast Pencil, 2011.

Thornton, Lucia. "What is Holistic Nursing?" *American Holistic Nurse Association.* 2015. http://ahna.org/About-Us/What-is-Holistic-Nursing

Vandross, Luther. "Here and Now." YouTube video. 5:18. August 27, 2011. https://www.youtube.com/watch?v=2iozIhNDrzQ.

Virtue, Doreen. *Archangels and Ascended Masters: A Guide to Working and Healing with Divinities and Deities.* New York: Hay House, 2004.

Virtue, Doreen. *The Angel Therapy Handbook.* New York: Hay House, 2011.

Wahls, Terry. *The Wahls Protocol: A Radical New Way to Treat All Autoimmune Conditions Using Paleo Principles.* New York: Avery, 2014.

What is Art Therapy?" *American Art Therapy Association.* 2013. http://www.arttherapy.org/upload/whatisarttherapy.pdf.

"What is Art Therapy?" *Brain Injury Alliance of Colorado.* December 10, 2014. http://biacolorado.org/art-therapy-classes/.

"What is Music Therapy?" *American Music Therapy Association.* Accessed 2015. http://www.musictherapy.org/about/musictherapy/.

Williams, Margery. *The Velveteen Rabbit.* New York: John H. Doran Company, 1922.

York III, George K., and David A. Steinberg. "Hughlings Jackson's Neurological Ideas." *Brain: A Journal of Neurology 134*, no. 10 (2011): 3106–3113. Accessed September 8, 2011. http://brain.oxfordjournals.org/content/134/10/3106.

A B O U T   T H E   A U T H O R

In May of 2008, Bridgid suffered traumatic brain injury
following a bicycle accident. She
re-learned basic life skills and
continues to be challenged by her
disabilities. Frustratingly, she had
to let go of her meaningful career
as an Advanced Registered Nurse
Practitioner. Bridgid has created a
large part of her healing journey
through restoring and re-defining
herself and is now focusing her
energy on sharing her story. She
has successfully presented nation-

ally and internationally and has appeared on TV, radio and
published in both articles and books. She shares eye-opening
and essential education, growth, and perspective to healthcare
providers as well as hope and inspiration to anyone suffering from traumatic injury and their advocates. She fills one's
mind, body and spirit with restoration. Attendees are amazed,
uplifted, inspired and surrounded with hope and reassurance.

CPSIA information can be obtained
at www.ICGtesting.com
Printed in the USA
LVOW05s1427240117
522001LV00025B/297/P